BE
WHAT
YOU
ARE

Be what you are

WARREN W. WIERSBE

 Tyndale House Publishers, Inc.
WHEATON, ILLINOIS

All Scripture quotations, unless otherwise noted,
are from the King James Version of the Bible.
Other versions quoted are *The Holy Bible,* New
International Version (NIV), copyright 1973, 1978,
1984 by the New York International Bible Society,
and *The Open Bible,* New King James Version
(NKJV), copyright 1982 by Thomas Nelson, Inc.

First printing, October 1988

Library of Congress Catalog Card Number 88-51104
ISBN 0-8423-0376-6
Copyright 1988 by Warren W. Wiersbe
All rights reserved
Printed in the United States of America

Dedicated with much appreciation
to three choice friends
in Christian publishing
who are very patient and
who encourage me to do my best:
Wendell Hawley, *Tyndale House*
Victor Oliver, *Oliver-Nelson Books*
Mark Sweeney, *Victor Books*

CONTENTS

CHAPTER 1

A Child in God's Family

T hat cynical deviser of definitions, Ambrose Bierce, once said that human birth was "the first and direct of all disasters." I find no record that Mr. and Mrs. Bierce had a family, so we can't blame what he said on their children. Perhaps it was the neighbor's children that made Ambrose write such a depressing definition.

However, there is a sense in which human birth does share in a "great disaster" because each of us is born with a sinful nature. It doesn't take new parents long to discover this sad fact about their little darlings. "Behold, I was shapen in iniquity," confessed King David, "and in sin did my mother conceive me" (Ps. 51:5).

The "great disaster" occurred when our first parents disobeyed God and plunged the whole human race into sin (Gen. 3; Rom. 5:12-21). God made us in his image (Gen. 1:27), but we are also born in Adam's image (Gen. 5:3); and that makes us sinners. The Old Testament story reveals how sinful we really are because it is "the book of the generations of Adam" (Gen. 5:1). When we were born, we were born into "the Adam family," which is the same as saying, we were born with a sinful nature (Eph. 2:1-3).

But that's not the end of the story. The Old Testament

may be "the book of the generations of Adam," but the New Testament opens with, "The book of the generation of Jesus Christ" (Matt. 1:1). After our first parents fell, *God in his grace started a new family!* It is possible for you and me—Adam's sinful descendants—to be born again and start a brand new life! The first Adam brought sin and condemnation into the human race, but the Last Adam, Jesus Christ (1 Cor. 15:45) brought righteousness and salvation. The good news of the gospel is that sinners may be forgiven and experience the miracle of being born again into the family of God through personal faith in Jesus Christ.

Let's examine three aspects of this miracle of the new birth and discover what it means to be a child in God's family.

1. Entering the Family (John 3:1-16)

The only way to get into the human family is by birth, and the only way to get into God's family is by birth. "Except a man be born again, he cannot see [experience] the kingdom of God. . . . Ye must be born again" (John 3:3, 7). The term that theologians use for this experience is *regeneration,* which simply means "born again."

Two spiritual parents. Children must have parents; that is the only way to be born in this world. God's children have two *spiritual* parents: the Spirit of God (John 3:5) and the Word of God (1 Pet. 1:23-25). The miracle of the new birth takes place when the Spirit of God applies the Word of God to the mind and heart of the sinner, and this Word generates faith (Eph. 2:8-9). The sinner believes on Jesus Christ, receives new life, and is born again into the family of God (John 1:11-13).

But didn't Jesus say that we must be "born of water" as well as "born of the Spirit"? Does this mean that water baptism is necessary for salvation? The phrase "born of

water" probably does not refer to water baptism because
in the Bible, water baptism is associated with *death* and
not with *birth.* "Born of water" means physical birth,
what Nicodemus referred to in verse 4. "Born of water" is
the same as "born of the flesh" in verse 6. First, the physical birth; then the spiritual birth. Anyone who is acquainted with human birth knows that water is involved;
the baby is "born of water."¹

John 1:13 declares that the new birth is not the result of
our own efforts, sincere and religious as they may be. You
cannot be born again through your family connections
("blood"), or by means of the religious acts that you do
("the will of the flesh"), or the good works that others may
do to you or for you ("the will of man"). This marvelous
spiritual birth can come only from God. The Greek word
translated "again" in verses 3 and 7 also means "from
above" (see John 3:31 and 19:11). No earthly religious
ceremony can impart heavenly life. Water baptism is important as a testimony of what God has done for us (Acts
2:41; 10:47), but it does not save us from sin.

Spiritual travail. Human birth involves travail. We
thank God for all the modern scientific equipment in the
obstetrics ward of the hospital, but the mother must still
travail if the child is to be born. One doctor said to me,
"Never forget that mothers go down into the valley so that
their children can come into the world." A sobering
thought!

Our Lord Jesus Christ had to travail in death on the
cross so that we might experience new birth (Isa. 53:11;
John 3:14-16). The new birth is all of grace. It is free, but
it is not cheap. It is the most costly gift you could ever receive.

The "birthmarks" of God's children. Can a person *really know* that he or she is a child in God's family? Of
course! The First Epistle of John was written to assure believers that they are the children of God (1 John 5:11-13).

Seven times in this letter, the Apostle John uses the phrase "born of God." If you put these statements together, you discover four "birthmarks" of the true believer:
- practicing righteousness and not sin (2:29; 3:9)
- loving God and other believers (4:7; 5:1)
- overcoming the world (5:4)
- overcoming the devil (5:18)

John was not suggesting that God's children never sin. The tense of the verbs in 2:29 and 3:9 literally means "everyone that *practices* righteousness" and "does not *practice* sin." God does not want his children to sin at all (1 John 2:1); but if they do sin, he has made provision for their cleansing (1 John 1:9). Christians are not people who *are* sinless, but who *do* sin less. The "bent" of their life is toward godliness and obedience.

Along with these "birthmarks," the believer has the witness of God's Word (1 John 5:9-13) and the witness of God's Spirit (Rom. 8:9, 14-17). These two witnesses are like "spiritual birth certificates" that assure us we are God's own children.

2. Enjoying the Family

Our heavenly Father gives to us "richly all things to enjoy" (1 Tim. 6:17). To look at some Christians, you would never suspect that the word *enjoy* is even in the Bible! Well, it is; and those of God's children who really understand all that he has given them will radiate his joy through their lives. What blessings does the Father want his children to enjoy?

The family freedom (Rom. 8:12-18). This paragraph describes a special relationship with the Father called "adoption," which must not be confused with adoption in the Western world. In the New Testament, adoption is the act of God whereby he gives each of his children an adult standing in the family the instant he or she is born again. You do not get into God's family by adoption but by regeneration. Why? Because an adopted child *does not have the same nature* as his adoptive parents. God's children have God's own nature because they have been born of God's Spirit (2 Pet. 1:4). Adoption has to do with our standing in the family. It simply means that God treats us as adults, not as babes, and gives us adult privileges.

For example, a baby does not even know he is a baby, and he certainly does not know his own parents. Even if a baby did know his own father, he would not be able to speak to him. But God's children know they are God's children! They not only know who their Father is, but they are able to speak to him and call him "Abba [Papa], Father!" For the most part, children live in bondage and fear until they are old enough to care for themselves; but God's children are free from both bondage and fear.

Why does God adopt his children and give them an adult standing in the family? So that they will have the freedom to draw upon all his resources and grow into mature sons and daughters. We are free to walk with him and talk with him, free to hear his Word and follow his Spirit. Even though we constantly need to grow, we do so in a family atmosphere of freedom and grace, not bondage and law.

The family food. If children are to grow, they must have food; and God has provided his Word as our spiritual nourishment (Jer. 15:16; Job 23:12). God's Word is bread (Matt. 4:4), milk (1 Pet. 2:2), meat (Heb. 5:12-14; 1 Cor. 3:1-2), and honey (Ps. 119:103). As we meditate on God's Word, the truth is "digested" inwardly and we receive strength (Josh. 1:6-9). When we are babes, we receive the Word from others who have "digested" it for us (1 Thess. 2:7-8); but as we grow spiritually, we learn to feed ourselves and enjoy the full diet of the Word. We can enjoy the "meat" as well as the "milk."

The family fortune. When we were born the first time ("born of the flesh"), we were born poor slaves; but when we were born the second time ("born of the Spirit"), we were born rich sons. It is the contrast between Abraham's two sons, Ishmael and Isaac, the slave and the heir (see Gal. 4:21-31). If we were treated as babies in the family of God, we could never inherit our wealth; but because God has given his children an adult standing, we can claim his wealth and use it for his glory. We are "heirs of God" (Rom. 8:15-17).

What kind of wealth does the Father share with us? Let us start with "the riches of his grace" (Eph. 2:7), keeping in mind that our Father is "the God of all grace" (1 Pet. 5:10), our Bible is "the word of his grace" (Acts 20:32), and the Holy Spirit is "the Spirit of grace" (Heb. 10:29). God's throne used to be a throne of judgment to us, but now it is a "throne of grace" where we can "find grace to help in time of need" (Heb. 4:16). "From the fullness of his grace we have all received one blessing after another" (John 1:16, NIV). That is why it is important that God's children study God's Word and get to know all the grace that is available to them through Jesus Christ.

Not only do we share the riches of his grace, but we also have the "riches of his mercy" (Eph. 2:4). There is a difference between *grace* and *mercy*. God in his mercy does not give us what we do deserve, and God in his grace gives us what we don't deserve. "It is of the Lord's mercies that we are not consumed" (Lam. 3:22). God's children experience "goodness and mercy" each day of their lives (Ps. 23:6).

Spiritual commodities like "grace" and "mercy" may seem rather nebulous to us, especially when it comes to paying our bills and keeping life going. God knows our daily needs and has provided for us "the riches of his glory." The promise to claim is Philippians 4:19, "But my God shall supply all your need according to his riches in glory by Christ Jesus." God does not satisfy our "greeds," but he does supply our needs (Matt. 6:19-34).

"The riches of his wisdom" are available when God's children must make decisions (Rom. 11:33). It is important to have knowledge, especially knowledge of the Word of God; but we also need wisdom in order to use that knowledge correctly. "If any of you lacks wisdom, he should ask God, who gives generously to all without finding fault, and it will be given to him" (James 1:5, NIV).

Finally, God's children draw upon "the riches of his goodness" (Rom. 2:4). "For the Lord is good" (Ps. 100:5). "Oh how great is thy goodness, which thou hast laid up for them that fear thee; which thou hast wrought for them that trust in thee before the sons of men!" (Ps. 31:19). God is the source of every good and perfect gift (James 1:17), and we can trust him to give what is right, in the right way, and at the right time.

No matter how you look at it, God's children are rich indeed!

The family fellowship. As children in God's family, we belong to each other and we need each other. God doesn't want his children to live in isolation (see Eccles. 4:9-12). This is one reason why our Lord established his church on earth: it is a living fellowship in which his children can worship him unitedly, witness of his grace, and encourage one another in the things of eternity. In the Greek language, the word *fellowship* means "to have in common"; and the children of God have much in common. They share the same life, the same Word, the same love for Christ, the same concern for a lost world, and the same desire to glorify God.

One of the first symptoms of a weakening fellowship with the Father is a believer's carelessness about fellowship with God's people. "Not forsaking the assembling of ourselves together" is a commandment from God (Heb. 10:25), and we should obey it. The first Christians "continued steadfastly in the apostles' doctrine and fellowship, and in the breaking of bread, and in prayers" (Acts 2:42).

Fellowship means that we are concerned about one another. In fact, the phrase "one another" is used nearly fifty times in the New Testament to describe how believers should minister to each other. "Love one another" is repeated at least a dozen times (John 23:34-35; 15:12, 17;

Rom. 13:8; 1 Thess. 3:12; 4:9). But we are also commanded to submit to one another (Eph. 5:21), encourage one
another (1 Thess. 4:18), care for one another (1 Cor.
12:25), forgive one another (Eph. 4:32), and edify one another (Rom. 14:19; 15:2), to name but a few. Fellowship
involves sharing ourselves with others. "The only basis for
real fellowship with God and man," wrote Roy Hession,
"is to live out in the open with both" (*The Calvary Road*,
p. 22).

The family fashions. God's children have taken off the
filthy garments of sin and have put on the garments of
God's grace, the righteousness of Jesus Christ (2 Cor. 5:21;
Isa. 61:10; 64:6). We have "put off the old man with his
deeds; and have put on the new man which is renewed in
knowledge after the image of him that created him" (Col.
3:9-10). Colossians 3:1-14 describes the "family fashions"
for the Christian, the garments of grace that the inner person ought to be wearing. Just as Jesus commanded the
grave clothes to be removed from Lazarus (John 11:44), so
should we put off by faith the grave clothes of the old life.
After all, we share God's life—and nobody will believe we
are alive if we don't dress like it!

The family future. God's family is the only family that
has a future hope, for there is no hope for the wicked sinners in Adam's family (Eph. 2:12). We have a living hope
(1 Pet. 1:4) because we trust a living Christ. He is preparing a home in heaven for his people, and he will return to
take us there (John 14:1-6). One day we shall see him and
become like him (1 John 3:1-3)! Nobody knows when the
Lord will return, but when he does, he will gather his
family together, the living and the dead, and take them to
glory (1 Thess. 4:13-18). What a future!

When you consider the joys that God's children can experience—and we haven't begun to consider all of them—
you wonder at two things: why more Christians aren't re-
joicing in their wonderful position in the family and why
more unsaved people aren't anxious to get into the family

and start enjoying abundant life in Christ. Perhaps if the children of God were more satisfied and joyful, the children of this world might want to trust Christ and be born again. How we live is as much a witness as what we say.

3. Enlarging the Family

God wants his family to grow. And his children don't have to be "mature" in order to start witnessing for Christ and pointing others to the Savior. New believers may not be ready to serve as teachers or spiritual leaders in the church (1 Tim. 3:6), but they can be faithful witnesses who share the gospel (Acts 1:8).

A witness is simply somebody who tells what he has seen or heard (Acts 4:19-20). I have been called to witness in court only a few times, but each time I discovered very quickly that the judge was not interested in my opinions on the case. All he wanted me to do was to tell what I really knew from my own personal experience. Too many Christians think they are prosecuting attorneys or judges, when God has called all of us to be witnesses.

There is a sense in which the child of God becomes a "spiritual father" by bringing others into the family of God (1 Cor. 4:15). As we share the Word of God and trust the Spirit of God, sinners get convicted and receive Jesus Christ personally. We may not always have the privilege of personally leading each one to Christ, but we can prepare the way for others. Witnessing is like farming—it is a cooperative effort. One plows, one sows, one waters, but God is the one who bring forth the harvest (1 Cor. 3:6-9; John 4:31-38).

It is interesting to examine the statistics recorded in the Book of Acts. About 120 believers met in the upper room for prayer after our Lord's ascension (Acts 1:15). Three thousand were converted at Pentecost (2:41), and later the number grew to be about five thousand (4:4). Day by day, believers were added to the Lord (5:14), so much so that the apostles had to appoint assistants to help them (6:1ff.). "And the word of God increased; and the number of disciples multiplied in Jerusalem greatly; and a great company of the priests were obedient to the faith" (6:7).

If we are to help enlarge God's family through our witness, we must first of all be sure that we are filled with the Spirit of God; because it is only through his power that our witnessing glorifies God and brings true conviction to sinners (Acts 1:8; John 16:8-11). While God certainly wants us to share our personal experience of salvation, he can use that experience only as it is related to the Word of God and as it magnifies the Son of God.

Second, we must sincerely desire to win the lost. Witnessing for Christ is not something we turn on and off, like a TV set. Every believer is a witness at all times—either a good one or a bad one. A burden for the lost keeps us asking God to make us good witnesses for Jesus Christ. If we start each day yielding ourselves to the Lord (Rom. 12:1-3) and seeking his blessing, he will use us to share the gospel with others.

It is important to remember that we are to be *witnesses*, not prosecuting attorneys. A member of one of the churches I pastored felt it was his duty to rebuke people who smoked in public, telling them that smoking was a filthy habit as well as a nuisance to others. Then he would tell them that Jesus would give them victory over the habit if they would get saved. Finally, I gently reminded him that even if these people *did* stop smoking, they were still lost and needed to trust Christ. I am not an encourager of smoking, but my friend was attempting to get people convicted about the wrong thing.

This leads to the third suggestion. As witnesses, we must keep in constant fellowship with the Lord so that we have something fresh to share. The Holy Spirit testifies to us through the Word so that we may bear witness joyfully (John 15:26-27). If we are prepared, we can then use these opportunities wisely when he opens the way. It isn't necessary to have a "canned sales talk" all ready. The Spirit can give us the words we need when we need them, if we are praying and walking in the Spirit. The new Christian may want to borrow a step-by-step plan when he or she first begins to witness, but it will not be long before that believer will become adept at sharing Christ as the Spirit directs. Jesus adapted his approach as he witnessed to people and we should follow his example.

Fourth, we need to "follow up" the new believers and help them grow in the Lord. After all, that is what any family is for—to love, protect, and nurture the new babies so they can successfully mature. The pastor especially, as a "spiritual father," sometimes needs to warn the children (1 Cor. 4:14), discipline them (1 Cor. 4:17-21), encourage them (1 Thess. 2:10-12), feed them (1 Cor. 3:1-3), and protect them from false teachers (2 Cor. 11:1-5). This is not an easy job, and each member of the family needs to help.

Three Questions

Have you entered the family of God, and do you have full assurance that you are his child?

Are you enjoying being in his family as you draw upon all the privileges that are yours in Christ?

Are you helping to enlarge the family by witnessing for Christ as the Lord gives you opportunity?

NOTES

[1]Sincere Bible students disagree on the meaning of "born of water." Some see water as a symbol of the Word of God (Eph. 5:26), but it is doubtful that Nicodemus would have understood that image, and Jesus expected him to understand (see John 3:10). Some translate the verse "born of water, *even* the Spirit," and this is permissible. However, I prefer the explanation given on page 13.

CHAPTER 2

A Sheep in God's Flock

I was raised in the asphalt jungles of the city where people think more about cats and dogs than they do about sheep. I don't recall ever seeing a sheep until I was in the third grade and our teacher took our class to visit a farm. I note that today some metropolitan zoos have model farm exhibits to help city children get acquainted with the animals they read about in storybooks. An excellent idea!

But people in Bible times needed no special exhibits to teach them about sheep. If you visit the Holy Land today, you may see flocks of sheep and goats even within the city limits. My wife and I once met a charming Jewish lad in Jerusalem who was caring for some sheep right in a city park! On one occasion our tour bus had to stop while a couple of shepherd lads led their flock across the highway. I wondered to myself what would happen if those lads tried to lead that flock across a busy street in Chicago. I concluded it would probably result in a surplus of mutton and lamb chops in the city markets.

"I think we've got to stop using the image of sheep when we talk about Christians," a preacher friend once said to me. "Today's sophisticated urban population may not know what we're talking about!"

But I think my friend is wrong. A person doesn't have to be a farmer to know what sheep are like or what they symbolize. William J. Lederer wasn't afraid to call his popular book *A Nation of Sheep*; and the Apostle Paul used the image of the flock when he addressed the church leaders from the great city of Ephesus (Acts 20:28-29). These elders were working in a sophisticated urban center, yet Paul reminded them that they were ministering to God's sheep. My own conviction is that we need to *emphasize* this image, not abandon it; because if we really understand what it means to be a sheep in God's flock, we will better be able to relate to each other, to our church leaders, and to our Lord.

1. Israel, God's Flock
The Jewish nation prided itself on being God's special flock. Jehovah God is called "the Shepherd of Israel" (Ps. 80:1), and the nation is "his people, and the sheep of his pasture" (Ps. 100:3). When God delivered Israel from Egypt, he led them "like a flock by the hand of Moses and Aaron" (Ps. 77:20; and see 78:52). When God called David to become Israel's king, he chose an experienced shepherd (Ps. 78:70-72). When the nation was in decline under King Ahab, the prophet Micaiah "saw all Israel scattered upon the hills, as sheep that have not a shepherd" (1 Kings 22:17, and see Mark 6:34). As he contemplated the Babylonian captivity, the prophet Jeremiah wept when he saw the "Lord's flock . . . carried away captive" (13:17).

The people of Israel saw God as their Shepherd and their own leaders as "under shepherds" who received authority from God to care for the flock. The great concern of Moses was that God would appoint a man to be his successor so that somebody dependable would lead the flock

(Num. 27:15-23). Priests and kings were looked upon as God's shepherds, even though some of them were not faithful in their "pastoral work." Jeremiah condemned the "pastors" (religious and political leaders) who destroyed the flock instead of serving it (23:1ff.; 25:34-38), and the prophet Ezekiel delivered a similar message to the "false shepherds" of his day (Ezek. 34). Even Cyrus, the "heathen" Persian king, was called a shepherd (Isa. 44:28).

In these modern days of dictatorships and democracies, it is difficult for us to believe that government leaders are God's shepherds. There are times when some people in office seem more like hirelings or even thieves (John 10:1-13). Israel was God's elect people, and no nation today can claim the privileges that Israel enjoyed, particularly God's special presence and his covenant blessings. Today those privileges belong to his church scattered around the world. Human government is ordained of God, and we must respect those in office, even if we disagree with them (Rom. 13; 1 Pet. 2:11-17). But if God could accomplish his purposes through a shepherd like Cyrus, certainly he can work through men and women in office today. Our responsibility is to pray for them (1 Tim. 2:1-4) and to submit to their leadership so long as we can maintain a good conscience toward God (1 Pet. 2:11-17; 3:8-22).

Israel was often a flock that went astray and disobeyed the Lord. "All we like sheep have gone astray" (Isa. 53:6) was first said about Israel, although it certainly applies to sinners in every nation (1 Pet. 2:25). Jesus saw the Jewish people as lost sheep, and he looked upon them with compassion (Matt. 9:36). In fact, he even died for them. "For the transgression of my people was he stricken" (Isa. 53:8). When he was here on earth, Jesus ministered to "the lost sheep of the house of Israel" (Matt. 10:6, 15). Today, the people of Israel are scattered throughout the world, but one day the Lord will regather his flock and give them his Shepherd to care for them (Ezek. 37:15-28; Matt. 2:6, where *rule* means "shepherd").

2. The Church, God's Flock

What Israel was under the old covenant, the church is today under the new covenant: "But ye are a chosen generation, a royal priesthood, an holy nation, a peculiar people
[a people of his own possession]" (1 Pet. 2:9; and note
Matt. 21:43). God has certainly not abandoned Israel
(Rom. 11:1), but in this present age, he is working in and
through his church to get the gospel to every creature. The
church is his "little flock" (Luke 12:32) made up of "lost
sheep" that the Good Shepherd has rescued (Matt.
18:10-14).

Why does God compare his people to sheep?

Sheep are "clean" animals (Lev. 11:1-8). This means they
are acceptable to God. Of course, no sinner is acceptable
in himself; our acceptance comes only through the merits
of Jesus Christ the Savior (2 Cor. 5:21; Eph. 1:6). But unlike dogs and pigs that often identify with filth (2 Pet. 2:20-
22), sheep prefer the green pastures and the still waters.
The nature of a creature determines its appetite, and it is
the nature of sheep to desire the pasture and not the gar-
bage dump. "Let everyone that nameth the name of Christ
depart from iniquity" (2 Tim. 2:19).

Sheep know their shepherd. Jesus said, "I am the good
shepherd, and know my sheep, and am known of mine"
(John 10:14). The Eastern shepherd has an intimate relationship with his sheep and knows their names (John 10:3,
27) and their personal characteristics and needs. He can
actually call them by name the way you and I might call a
child or a pet dog. The sheep know the shepherd's voice
and obey it, but they will not follow if they hear another
voice (John 10:3-4).

There are many voices calling to us today, and some of
them even sound "religious." But a true child of God will
not follow when he hears the voice of strangers (John
10:5). God's voice to us today is the Word of God, taught
by the Spirit of God (Rev. 2:7, 11, 17). Any professed
"shepherd" that denies this Word is a false shepherd, a

thief and a robber, and is dangerous to the flock. False prophets are "wolves in sheep's clothing" (Matt. 7:15) who will entice Christ's sheep if they can.

It is encouraging to realize that Christ knows each of his sheep by name. Remembering names has always been a problem for me, and I never quite know how to reply when somebody approaches me and says, "Hi! Do you remember me?" Our Lord doesn't have that problem, and we don't have to wear name tags to help him recognize us. We may be statistics and numbers as far as the world's computers are concerned, but we are precious individuals as far as our Shepherd is concerned. He knows his sheep personally.

Sheep desperately need a shepherd. For the most part, sheep are defenseless animals, easily frightened, and quickly led astray. Unlike predatory beasts, or even cattle, sheep need someone to guide them and guard them or they will get into trouble. Without the loving care of the shepherd, the sheep would be helpless. "O Lord, I know that the way of man is not in himself; it is not in man that walketh to direct his steps" (Jer. 10:23). Why? Jeremiah gives us the answer: "The heart is deceitful above all things, and desperately wicked: who can know it?" (17:9). Unless we follow our Shepherd, we will soon go astray (1 Pet. 2:25).

Just as the people of Israel had undershepherds to direct the affairs of the nation, so the local church has pastors to give spiritual direction and protection to the flock (Eph. 4:11). The English word *pastor* comes from the Latin word *shepherd,* and it is equivalent to "elder" and "bishop" or "overseer" (Acts 20:17, 28). The local pastor holds a responsible position before God and the people, and his ministry is not to be taken lightly. It is not a job for a novice or for one who does not possess the qualifications given in Scripture (1 Tim. 3:1-7; Titus 1:5-9). So long as the pastor obeys the Word and follows the Lord, the sheep should follow him (1 Cor. 11:1; Heb. 13:7-8, 17).

Sheep are useful animals. In Bible times, the shepherd did not keep his flock in order to slaughter them, because meat was a luxury to the Jews. He wanted his sheep alive since he profited from their wool as well as from their young. Sheep were killed for Passover and festive family occasions and sometimes for sacrifices to the Lord. But for the most part, the sheep were protected as part of the family wealth. The loss of a lamb or a sheep was a costly thing to a family.

Certainly the Good Shepherd has every right to expect his sheep to be useful to him. "Who feedeth a flock, and eateth not of the milk of the flock?" (1 Cor. 9:7). In return for all that he gives to us and does for us, we as God's sheep ought to be giving our very best to him. It is good for sheep to be shorn and to produce young. Christ's sheep should be "living sacrifices," ready to do his will no matter what the price may be (Rom. 8:36; 12:1-2). If all we do is enjoy the "green pastures" and "still waters" (Ps. 23:2), and do nothing to serve him, then we are indeed selfish and useless.

Sheep flock together. It is the nature of sheep to want to be with the flock, and it is the nature of believers to want to be with one another. The New Testament knows nothing of isolated Christian living. In those days when a person trusted Christ, he let it be known by identifying himself with other believers. The isolated sheep is not only in danger but is also dangerous because he could lead other sheep astray. The place of safety, sufficiency, and service is with God's flock.

3. Christ, the Shepherd

The Bible presents the shepherding ministry of Jesus Christ from three different perspectives. As the Good Shepherd, he died for the sheep (John 10:11, 15, 17-18); as the Great Shepherd, he lives for the sheep to perfect them (Heb. 13:20-21); and as the Chief Shepherd, he will return to gather his sheep and take them to heaven (1 Pet. 5:1-4). These three shepherd titles encompass his ministry to us in the past, present, and future.

Bible students have noticed that there is a parallel between the three shepherd titles of the Lord and Psalms 22, 23, and 24. Psalm 22 describes the Good Shepherd who gives his life for the sheep. Psalm 23 tells us of the Great Shepherd's provision and protection for his sheep, his ministry to us "all the days of our lives." Psalm 24 is a victory psalm that announces the arrival of the King, the Chief Shepherd, who will defeat his enemies and reward his people.

The Good Shepherd (John 10; Ps. 22). When Jesus called himself a "shepherd," he identified himself with a group of men who were, for the most part, rejected in the society of that day. One of the Jewish commentaries on Psalm 23 says, "No position in the world is so despised as that of the shepherd." Shepherds were classified with thieves. Pious Jews would not do business with shepherds, and judges would not ask shepherds to give testimony in court. Yet Jesus called himself a shepherd. Indeed, he is the friend of the outcasts (Luke 5:27-32; 15:1-2).

The word *good* carries with it the idea of "beautiful, noble, blameless." Many great men in Scripture were shepherds—Abel, the first martyr; the Patriarchs; David—but none is greater than Jesus Christ, the Son of God. In the Old Testament, the sheep died for the shepherd; but under the new covenant, the Shepherd died for the sheep. Jesus was not murdered or martyred. He *willingly* gave his life for the sheep. The blood of sheep could never adequately deal with man's sins, but the blood of Christ finished the work of redemption completely (Heb. 10:1-14).

But if we, God's people, are sheep, isn't there a danger that we might wander away and be lost? Not when Jesus Christ is our Good Shepherd! To begin with, when we trust him, we receive *eternal* life; and that in itself assures us of safety and security. Also, this eternal life is *a gift*. It is not something we earn by our good works. If we can't be saved by our good works, then how can we be lost by our bad works? Furthermore, the Lord gives us his promise, "They shall never perish" (John 10:28-29). If we do stray away from him, we can be sure that he will seek us and bring us back to the flock and the fold. This assurance is not an excuse for sin and disobedience, but it is an encouragement when Satan accuses us and tells us we have no hope because we have disobeyed the Shepherd. "I have gone astray like a lost sheep; seek thy servant; for I do not forget thy commandments" (Ps. 119:176).

As the Good Shepherd, Jesus Christ willingly died for the sheep a terrible death that is described in Psalm 22:1-21. (Verses 22-31 relate to his resurrection; see Heb. 2:12.) We can almost see the rebellious mob gathered about the cross, like so many wild animals. And we can almost hear their shouts of mockery and contempt. But the Good Shepherd did not return their insults (1 Pet. 2:18-23). Instead, he prayed for them and asked the Father to forgive them (Luke 23:34).

The Great Shepherd (Heb. 13:20-21; Ps. 23). As the Good Shepherd, our Lord finished the work of redemption and on the cross *purchased* his people (John 17:4; 19:30). Then, he returned to the Father in heaven and took up his new ministry as the Great Shepherd, who *perfects* his people. What is Jesus doing in heaven today? He is ministering as the believer's High Priest (Heb. 4:14-16; 8:1-2) and Advocate (1 John 2:1-2). He is reigning from a throne of grace, not a throne of judgment; and he is seeking to work in us and through us to accomplish his perfect will.

The phrase "make you perfect" in Hebrews 13:21 is a translation of the Greek word *katartidzo,* an unfamiliar word to most people today, but very familiar to the Greek-speaking people in the early church. To the soldiers it meant "to equip an army for battle," and to the sailors, "to outfit a ship for a voyage." In medical circles it meant "to set a broken bone" or "to adjust a limb"; and among fishermen it meant "to mend the nets" (Matt. 4:21). These beautiful shades of meaning help us understand what the Great Shepherd wants to do in our lives.

To begin with, he wants to equip us for battle and outfit us for the voyages of life. How foolish is that soldier who goes to battle without his armor, or that sailor who sets sail without first getting the ship ready for the voyage! As he ministers from heaven, our Great Shepherd wants to "set the broken bones" in our spiritual lives and adjust us as members of his body, the church. He seeks to "mend" us so that he can use us as effective "fishers of men."

What tools does the Lord use to perfect us? Primarily, he uses the Word of God (2 Tim. 3:16-17) and the fellowship of the local church (Eph. 4:11-16). But he also uses prayer (1 Thess. 3:10) and even suffering (1 Pet. 5:10). Each believer should be available to the Lord to help perfect other believers who have failed (Gal. 6:1). The purpose of church discipline is to reclaim the offender, not destroy him. It is like setting a broken bone in the body of Christ—and that requires patience and tenderness.

The purpose of this perfecting ministry is *service for him*. We don't grow in grace just so that we can be on exhibition and get the praises of people. Remember, we are sheep, not statues. And we are supposed to be useful to the Shepherd. He wants to work *in* us so that he can work *through* us and accomplish his will on earth. If our personal sanctification doesn't result in service to others and glory to God, then it is mere religious piety.

Psalm 23 is often read at funerals, mainly because of the comforting promise found in verse 4; but the psalm really describes what the Great Shepherd does for us "all the days of [our] life" (v. 6). It explains that the Lord's ministry to his sheep is for the present as well as the future, and that what he does is for the days of our life as well as the hour of our death. The psalm begins with a great affirmation—"The Lord is my shepherd"—and then points out two assurances based on this affirmation: "I shall not

want" and "I will fear no evil." Because the Lord is our
Great Shepherd, we have provision (vv. 1-3) and protection
(vv. 4-6), sufficiency and security.

As his sheep, we may not always understand what the
Shepherd is doing, but we know we can trust him. Whether in the pastures, beside the pools, or on the paths, he is
caring for us and meeting our every need. Why? "For his
name's sake" (v. 3). All that he does for his sheep is for the
glory of his name. (See Eph. 1:6, 12, 14.) Our Lord has
more to lose than we do if ever he should fail. We don't see
it now, but one day in glory we shall look back and see
that "goodness and mercy" have followed us all the days of
our lives! This is David's version of Romans 8:28.

The Good Shepherd *died* for the sheep and the Great
Shepherd *lives* for the sheep, to protect them, perfect them,
and direct them. The Good Shepherd gave his life *for* the
sheep, and the Great Shepherd gives his life *to* the sheep.
They have eternal life and abundant life (John 10:10, 28),
security and sufficiency. All the sheep must do is stay close
to the Shepherd and follow him, listening to his voice and
obeying what he says.

The Chief Shepherd (1 Pet. 5:4; Ps. 24). One day the
Chief Shepherd will return, gather his sheep, and take
them to heaven. He will come as the King of Glory, defeat
all his foes, and establish his kingdom. He will reward his
faithful undershepherds with a crown of glory that will
never fade away. While not all Christians agree on the details of prophetic events, they do agree on the promise of
his coming, and they pray for it and live expectantly. When
we see Jesus Christ, we will enter into the full experience
of "one fold, and one shepherd" (John 10:16).

We will still be his precious sheep in heaven, for "the
Lamb which is in the midst of the throne shall feed [shep-
herd] them, and shall lead them unto living fountains of
waters: and God shall wipe away all tears from their eyes"
(Rev. 7:17). In his righteous kingdom, "he shall rule [shep-
herd] them [the nations] with a rod of iron" (Rev. 19:15).

Psalm 24 depicts our Lord as the victorious warrior and the glorious King, and we shall reign with him.

Meanwhile, as his sheep, purchased by his blood, we have some responsibilities to fulfill.

First, we must keep alert to the voice of the Shepherd as he speaks to us in his Word (John 10:3-5). We will not hear an audible voice telling us what to do. But we can discover his leading as we study the Bible, meditate, pray, and obey what he reveals to us. We must follow him a step at a time and live for him a day at a time, letting him plan the future and prepare us for it.

Second, we must stay close to the Shepherd, no matter where he may lead us. He may guide us to the comfortable green pastures and the refreshing quiet waters. Or, he may lead us right into the dark valley. We must never permit our circumstances to frighten us or to distract us from watching him. Once we take our eyes of faith off the Shepherd, we will start to wander away. Someone has said, "Obstacles are those nasty things you see when you take your eyes off the Lord." How true!

Third, if we do stray, we must cry out for the Shepherd's help and trust him to restore us. Peter denied his Lord three times, but the Lord sought him out, forgave him, and restored him (Mark 16:7; Luke 24:34). In fact, he even commissioned Peter to shepherd his flock (John 21).

Fourth, we must be a part of the Lord's flock, following the spiritual leadership of his appointed shepherds. No flock is perfect, but each flock is important. Solitary sheep are always in danger, no matter how experienced they think they are. "Most people would not want to live where there are no churches," wrote Vance Havner, "but many of them live *as though* there were no churches." It is the nature of sheep to want to flock together.

Finally, we must be useful to the Shepherd. Not everyone is called of God to be a pastor, but each believer is called to minister the spiritual gifts that God has given him (1 Pet. 4:10). If each member of the flock is faithful to follow, care, and serve, the flock will be strong and will multiply. When we follow the Shepherd, we automatically get closer to the other sheep who are following him. And this should result in a greater love for each other and a better ministry to one another.

When Dr. Handley Moule was Bishop of Durham, he did something unusual for ministers in that day: he drove an automobile. The license number that happened to be assigned to his car was J1011. The Bishop "interpreted" this to mean John 10:11: "I am the good shepherd: the good shepherd giveth his life for the sheep."

Jesus Christ *is* the Good Shepherd, and the Great Shepherd, and the Chief Shepherd.

Are you one of his sheep?

CHAPTER 3

A Pilgrim Citizen

T wo of the most fascinating images of the Christian are the "pilgrim and stranger" and the "citizen of heaven." The concept that ties these two images together is just as fascinating, the believer's *calling* in Jesus Christ. Those who have trusted Christ as their Savior are "the called of Jesus Christ" (Rom. 1:6). They no longer belong to this present world system but are instead the citizens of heaven and pilgrims and strangers on the earth.

This calling has four different aspects.

1. Christians Are Called Out

The English word *ecclesiastical* comes from a Greek word *ekklesia*, which means "a called-out assembly." *Ekklesia* is a familiar New Testament word, used 114 times and usually translated "church." The church is God's "called out assembly." The Greeks applied the word *ekklesia* to their own local assemblies that transacted public business in the free cities. The *ekklesia* was made up of qualified citizens who were "called out" for the purpose of managing the affairs of the government.

God's approach. Ever since man first sinned, God has

been seeking lost sinners and calling to them to receive his forgiveness (Gen. 3:1-10; Luke 19:10). God does not call us because we deserve it. He calls us in grace because he loves us and longs to save us. Jesus said, "I came not to call the righteous, but sinners to repentance" (Mark 2:17). God is seeking sinners because sinners are certainly not seeking after God (Rom. 3:10-11). The initiative comes from the loving heart of God, not from the rebellious heart of man.

How does God go about calling lost sinners? Paul described the approach God takes:

But we are bound to give thanks always to God for you, brethren beloved of the Lord, because God hath from the beginning chosen you unto salvation through sanctification of the Spirit and belief of the truth: whereunto he called you by our gospel, to the obtaining of the glory of our Lord Jesus Christ. (2 Thess. 2:13-14)

Our calling began in eternity when God the Father chose us in Christ "before the foundation of the world" (Eph. 1:4). We had nothing to do with this decision. It was purely an act of God's grace. Christians are "elect according to the foreknowledge of God the Father" (1 Pet. 1:2). Jesus said, "Ye have not chosen me, but I have chosen you" (John 15:16). The lost sinner knows nothing about this eternal decision, *nor does he need to know*. Election is a sacred secret that belongs to God's people, and it should not be discussed among those who are not saved. What the unsaved need to hear is the good news of the gospel.

This leads us to the second step in God's gracious approach to winning the lost: he sends witnesses to share the good news of salvation. The same God who ordains the end (the salvation of the lost sinner) also ordains the means to the end (the sharing of the gospel message). Paul wrote, "He [God] called you by our gospel." Anyone who says, "Well, God will save his elect without my help!" doesn't understand either the gospel or God's plan of evangelism. "How then shall they call on him in whom they have not believed? and how shall they believe in him of whom they have not heard? and how shall they hear without a preacher?" (Rom. 10:14).

The third step involves the ministry of the Holy Spirit who convicts the sinner and reveals the Savior. The sinner believes the truth of the gospel and is saved. The sinner's decision is much more than an intellectual assent to certain religious propositions. It is a personal meeting with Jesus Christ, in the Word and through the Spirit, a meeting that results in the imparting of new life to the believing sinner. Through faith in Christ he becomes a child of God!

A review of 2 Thessalonians 2:13-14 shows that all three persons in the Trinity are involved in our calling. God the Father chose us, God the Son died for us, and God the Spirit convicted us and imparted new life when we trusted Christ. Before I was saved, I knew nothing about divine election. But after I became a Christian and started reading my Bible, I discovered to my amazement that God in his grace had chosen me long before I even knew him!

The beloved former pastor of the Moody Church in Chicago, Dr. Harry Ironside, used to illustrate this truth by describing a door. The sinner is standing outside the door and he reads above it, "Whosoever will, let him come!" He believes God's promise, steps through the door, and is saved. He then turns around and reads above the *inside* of the door, "Chosen in Christ before the foundation of the world."

It is important to see that the Godhead works together in the salvation of lost sinners. As far as God the Father is concerned, I was saved when he chose me in Christ before the foundation of the world. But I knew nothing about his choice. As far as God the Son is concerned, I was saved when he died for me on the cross. But what he did on the cross was not effective in my life until I yielded to the ministry of the Holy Spirit, and then it all came together and I was born into God's family.

The new standing. From what has the believer been called out? We have been called out of what the Bible calls "the world." Jesus said, "They are not of the world, even as I am not of the world" (John 17:16). But what does he mean by "the world"? Certainly not the material world or the world of people (see 1 Cor. 5:9-10). We have an important job to do, and we can't accomplish it by isolating ourselves from everybody else. By "the world," Jesus means *the present evil system that is behind the sins of this world.* "Society without God and against Jesus Christ" is one way to express it. "The world" is the present order of things, organized by Satan to oppose the work of the Lord (1 John 2:15-17).

In our daily conversation, we often use the word *world* to mean an invisible system that exerts influence. For example, when we talk about "the world of sports," "the world of finance," or "the world of politics," nobody ever dreams that we are referring to a special planet or a visible organization housed in an office. People know we are speaking metaphorically about a "system" that relates to sports, finance, and politics. When the Bible warns Christians about "the world," the phrase is used in that same sense, to describe an invisible but influential system of things that is opposed to God.

Our old citizenship was in "the world" (Eph. 2:1-3), but our new citizenship is "in heaven" (Phil. 3:20, where *conversation* in the King James Version means "citizenship"). God has called us out of death and into life (John 5:24-25), out of darkness and into light (1 Pet. 2:9), out of Satan's kingdom and into the kingdom of his Son (Col. 1:13), out of shame and into his wonderful glory (1 Pet. 5:10). We have a new position in Jesus Christ, and this new position determines our conduct (Col. 3:1ff.; Eph. 4:1ff.).

When it comes to the world system, God's children are

"strangers and pilgrims" (1 Pet. 1:1; 2:11). A stranger is *away from home*, but a pilgrim is *on the way home*. In Bible days, a "stranger" was a "resident alien" who lived alongside the people of a land but was not one of them. As pilgrims, we are like Abraham and the patriarchs who stepped out by faith and obeyed God's call (Heb. 11:8-16). Wherever Abraham went, he pitched his tent and built his altar (Gen. 12:7-8; 13:1-4, 18). Abraham was a wealthy man and could have lived in an elegant house, but that would have hindered him from moving on when God spoke. The tent reminded him that he was a stranger and pilgrim, and the altar reminded him that he was a citizen of heaven, looking for the promised city (Heb. 11:10, 14-16). It takes both if we are to be successful in our Christian pilgrimage.

All of us live in a "tent," a frail human body (2 Cor. 5:1-8). When a Christian dies, the tent is "taken down" and the spirit goes to be with Christ in heaven (Phil. 1:21-24). But while we are living *in* this world, we must be careful not to start living *like* this world or *for* this world. We must beware of loving what the world loves (1 John 2:15-17) and doing what the world does (Rom. 12:2). James 4:4 warns that "the friendship of the world is enmity with God." Of course, we must be friendly with the unsaved; otherwise we would not be able to witness to them; but we dare not get "spotted" by the world (James 1:27) or "entangled" with the world (2 Tim. 2:3-4). The unsaved are watching us, and we must live as those who are the citizens of heaven (1 Pet. 2:11-12). We must let our lights shine so the lost will want to trust the Savior and join us in our pilgrimage.

2. Christians Are Called Together

We must not get the idea that as "strangers and pilgrims" we are alone in this present evil world; for we are not only called *out*, but we are also called *together*. "And all that

believed were together" (Acts 2:44). "Not forsaking the assembling of ourselves together" (Heb. 10:25) is one of
God's commandments to his pilgrim people. Since we
share the same calling and are traveling toward the same
heavenly destiny, it is only right that we meet together and
minister to one another. All Christians need to heed the ad-
monition that old Jacob gave to his sons when they started
on their journey to Egypt, "Don't quarrel on the way!"
(Gen. 45:24, NIV).

Christian "politics." When Paul reminded the Philippians that their "citizenship" was in heaven (3:20), he
used the Greek word *politeuma,* which gives us the English word *politics.* (You will find the same word in Philippians 1:27.) This is significant because the city of Philippi
was actually a Roman colony. In order to help protect their
empire, the Romans settled some of their loyal citizens (often army veterans) in various cities and then governed
those cities the way the city of Rome was governed. A Roman colony was organized and controlled by Roman law,
and the citizens of the colony had the same privileges as
those who lived on Italian soil. It was a high honor for a
city to be named a colony, and the residents did all they
could to bring glory to the name of Rome.

Each local church is a "colony of heaven" on earth,
made up of people whose citizenship is in heaven because
their names are written down in heaven (Luke 10:20). In
Paul's day a person could acquire Roman citizenship by
birth or purchase (Acts 22:28), or by receiving it as a gift.
Christians are citizens of heaven because they have been
born again through faith in Christ. Their heavenly citizenship is a gift they have received, a gift purchased for them
by the blood of God's Son.

Roman citizenship was something to be proud of, for it
carried with it many privileges, such as holding public office, participating in the assemblies, inheriting property,
being protected by the law, and even having the privilege
of appealing to the emperor himself. But think of the privileges God's people have because of their heavenly citizen-

ship! We are protected by heaven's armies (Heb. 1:14; Ps. 34:7). We can speak to our King at any time. We can serve him. We share his riches and his authority as we minister on earth. And one day he will summon us to our heavenly home.

People who lived in Roman colonies had to remember that most outsiders would judge Rome by the way the colonists behaved. It was very important that the Philippians, for example, obey the law and honor the emperor, or they would bring disgrace to Rome. But the same principle applies to the church, God's "colony of heaven" on earth. People judge the Lord by the way we behave, and that is why it is essential that we conduct ourselves as it becomes the gospel of Jesus Christ (Phil. 1:27).

When the citizens of heaven come together, it should be to worship the Lord, encourage one another, and witness to the lost. How sad it is when church meetings are only "business as usual" instead of being marked by spiritual power and blessing! When unsaved people visit our services, can they easily tell that we are the citizens of heaven, or does the church behave just like people in the world?

I recommend that you study the "one another" verses in the New Testament and discover what God expects his people to do when they are called together. We are prone to take both the privileges and the responsibilities of church fellowship for granted, and this is what robs us of the excitement and enrichment of our Christian fellowship. The more we live as pilgrims and strangers and as the citizens of heaven, the greater will be our enjoyment of communion with God's chosen people. The nearer we are to the world, the less excited we become about being with the people of God.

3. Christians Are Called Forth

We have been called *out of* the world so that Christ might send us back *into* the world, in order that we might rescue others *from* the world. Jesus said to his Father, "As thou

hast sent me into the world, even so have I also sent them
into the world" (John 17:18). If we were still *of* the world,
we could not help the world. But because we no longer belong to this world system, we are free to lead others into
the joy of salvation through faith in Christ.

The Christian life is a pilgrimage from earth to heaven,
and our task is to take as many as possible with us as we
make this journey. We should be saying to those around us
what Moses said to his father-in-law: "We are setting out
for the place about which the Lord said, 'I will give it to
you.' Come with us and we will treat you well" (Num.
10:29, NIV).

We are called forth by the Lord to minister wherever he
leads us, and we must be prepared to obey. As citizens of
heaven, we are under his command. And as pilgrims on
earth, we must be careful to have no attachments that
would hold us back. Anything in our lives that hinders us
from hearing God's call and obeying it is worldly and must
be abandoned. We never know when God might call us. It
was during a worship service in Antioch that the Lord
called Saul (Paul) and Barnabas to leave home and carry
the gospel to the Gentiles. They were *called forth* by God
and *sent forth* by the Holy Spirit working through the
church (Acts 13:1-4), and they immediately obeyed.

The contrast between Abraham and Lot illustrates this
truth (Gen. 12–19). Abraham believed God and obeyed
when God called him from Ur of the Chaldees to go to a
land about which he knew nothing. God led Abraham a
step at a time, a day at a time; and wherever Abraham
went, he pitched his tent (a pilgrim and stranger) and
built his altar to God (a citizen of heaven). He was ready
to obey.

Lot, however, did not have the heart of a true pilgrim,
although he was a saved man (2 Peter 2:7). He became
fascinated with Sodom and started to move in that direction (Gen. 13:5-13). Abraham maintained his separated
position, but Lot eventually moved into Sodom and was
taken captive by the enemy (14:12). Abraham rescued his

backslidden nephew, but Lot went right back into Sodom again. When the angels visited Sodom, they found Lot sitting in the gate, which indicates that he was now an official in the city (19:1). Lot forsook the tent and the altar, and everything he lived for went up in smoke when God destroyed Sodom. He was saved "yet so as by fire" (1 Cor. 3:15).

During this present age, God is taking out a people for his name (Acts 15:14). He uses us to share the message with the lost, and it is important that we do our job faithfully, empowered by the Holy Spirit of God (Acts 1:8). While it is true that every believer has a ministry, no matter what his or her vocation may be, it is also true that God calls some of his pilgrims to serve in special ways. One foreign mission board for which I pray is today looking for more than four hundred volunteers to fill various places of ministry. There are also empty places to fill in our local churches. As God's pilgrims, we need to be praying that the Lord will send out laborers who will get his work done (Luke 10:1-2).

4. Christians Will One Day Be Called Up

Christians are the citizens of heaven. Therefore, the heavenly home is their destiny. The Savior is now preparing a place for each of us in the Father's house, and he has promised to return and take us to that wonderful home (John 14:1-6). When he will return, nobody knows, and it is dangerous to set dates (Luke 17:20-37).

Most Christians believe in what is called "the imminent return of Christ." The word *imminent* means "ready to take place." In other words, nothing special has to happen for the Lord to return. He may come today, or he may wait another generation. Since nobody knows when Jesus Christ will return, it behooves all of his people to be ready every hour of every day to meet their Lord.

Realizing that at any moment we may be "called up," we should concentrate on holy living (1 John 2:28–3:3) and faithful service (Matt. 25:14-30). Each believer's works will be judged at the judgment seat of Christ, and all faithful service will be generously rewarded by the Lord (Rom. 14:10-12; 2 Cor. 5:9-10). Those who have not been faithful will lose their reward. "If any man's work shall be burned, he shall suffer loss [of reward]: but he himself shall be saved; yet so as by fire" (1 Cor. 3:15). It is the servant who says, "My lord delays his coming" that gets into trouble (Luke 12:41-48).

Since our citizenship is in heaven and our home is in heaven, we as God's pilgrims must cultivate a "heavenly mind" as we journey here on earth. We must constantly be looking for the Savior (Phil. 3:20). This does not mean that we neglect our earthly responsibilities and, as D. L. Moody used to say, become "so heavenly minded that we are no earthly good." Quite the contrary is true. People who are looking for their Lord ought to be *more faithful* as parents, children, employees, citizens, friends, and servants of God.

It was this "heavenly hope" that motivated men of faith like Abraham, Isaac, and Jacob; for they "looked for a city . . . whose builder and maker is God" (Heb. 11:10; note vv. 13-16). The eyes of God's pilgrims must not look *back* to the old life (Luke 9:62), or look *around* at the distractions of the world (Gen. 13:10-11). They must focus *above*, by faith, and be fixed on the Lord Jesus Christ (Heb. 12:1-2). Because we have been raised with Christ, we should "seek those things which are above" (Col. 3:1ff.).

It is not easy to be one of God's faithful pilgrims, to live a separated life and be ready at all times to move as he commands. But the rewards are worth it. We not only enjoy his presence and blessing on earth, but we have the assurance of a wonderful future in heaven. We know that Christ has promised to return, and when he does, we will be "caught up . . . to meet the Lord in the air: and so shall we ever be with the Lord" (1 Thess. 4:17).

After all, you shouldn't mind being a pilgrim and stranger in this world when you know your destination is heaven.

A Member in Christ's Body

CHAPTER 4

Saul, Saul, why do you persecute me?"
When the exalted Lord Jesus Christ asked Saul that
question (Acts 9:4, NIV), he revealed a great truth. When
you lay hands on God's people, you lay hands on God's
Son. His people are united with him just as the members
of the body are united. Jesus Christ is "the head over everything for the church, which is his body, the fullness of him
who fills everything in every way" (Eph. 1:22-23, NIV), and
each Christian is a member of his body.

But what does this mean? What difference should it
make to us as believers that we are members of his body
and also "members one of another" (Rom. 12:5)? Five key
words help to summarize the answer: vitality, unity, diversity, maturity, and ministry. With each of these words there
comes a responsibility for each believer to fulfill to the glory of God.

1. Vitality
The believer's union with Jesus Christ is a *living* union.
When we trusted Jesus Christ as our Savior, the Spirit of
God gave us spiritual life and placed us into the body of

Christ. "For by one Spirit are we all baptized into one body, whether we be Jews or Gentiles, whether we be bond or free" (1 Cor. 12:13). Notice that we did not put ourselves into his body, nor did another believer do it for us by means of some religious ritual. This work was totally and solely accomplished by the Holy Spirit of God in response to our faith in Christ.

The word *baptized* in 1 Corinthians 12:13 confuses some people, and this is understandable because we usually associate the word with water. But the Greek word *baptizo* has both a literal and a figurative meaning. Literally, it means "to submerge, to immerse." Figuratively, it means "to be identified with." It is the figurative meaning that Paul used in 1 Corinthians 12:13. The Holy Spirit identified us with Christ and made us a part of his body when we trusted the Savior.

It is important to note that we do not baptize ourselves; it is the Spirit who does it. Also, every believer has this experience and it takes place only once, at the time of conversion. It is not a postconversion experience for a select group of "super saints." Paul said that *all* believers had been baptized, not just a few.

Paul never *commanded* believers to be baptized by the Spirit. He did admonish us to be filled with the Spirit, for that experience must be repeated as we seek to witness and serve the Lord (Eph. 5:18; Acts 2:4; 4:8, 31). To confuse the once-for-all baptism of the Spirit with the continual filling of the Spirit is to confuse salvation with service and our position in Christ with our power from Christ.

The witness of the Spirit within us is evidence that we are indeed God's children (Rom. 8:9, 16). How does the Spirit witness to us? For one thing, he speaks through the Word of God, illuminating its pages and teaching us its truths. He also witnesses to us through contacts with God's people as we worship and serve together. He gives us that sense of "belonging." We love God's people and want to be with them. The Spirit also witnesses *through us* and enables us to share Christ with the lost (Acts 1:8). This wit-ness is not something that we manufacture in our own power. The Spirit enables us to witness and do it in a way that is natural and not forced.

A Christian is not somebody who tries to imitate Christ. A Christian is a person who is identified with Christ as a member of his body and the life of Christ flows in and through him. He has a living relationship with the glori-fied Son of God through the indwelling Spirit of God (1 Cor. 6:19-20; Gal. 2:20). This means he can have a life of spiritual vitality as he draws upon the strength of the Lord. The "Spirit of life in Christ Jesus" (Rom. 8:2) enables him to obey the will of God and produce fruit for his glory (Gal. 5:22-23).

This brings us to the Christian's first responsibility: to maintain a close communion with the Lord so that Christ's life and power enable you in your walk, your work, your witness, and your spiritual warfare.

2. Unity
"There is one body" (Eph. 4:4). There are many local "church bodies" around the world, but all true believers are members of that one body of which Jesus Christ is the Head. As Christians, we may wear different denomination-al labels, but we all belong to Christ and to one another in a spiritual unity created by God. Our task is to endeavor "to keep [safeguard] the unity of the Spirit in the bond of peace" (Eph. 4:3).

In Ephesians 4:4-6 Paul listed the seven bonds that unite the people of God:
- *One body:* the church (Eph. 1:22-23)
- *One Spirit:* the Holy Spirit sent from the Father
- *One hope:* the return of Jesus Christ (Titus 2:13)
- *One Lord:* our Lord Jesus Christ (see 1 Cor. 12:3)
- *One faith:* the basic Christian doctrine given to the apos-tles (Jude 3; 1 Tim. 6:20-21)

- *One baptism:* the baptism of the Spirit
- *One God:* the Father of all

At this point, we must carefully distinguish between *unity* and *uniformity*. Unity comes from life within and is a living thing, while uniformity is something mechanical and manufactured. A company of soldiers in a parade are uniform in what they wear and do, but this uniformity is no proof they are experiencing unity. They may be angry at their commander and perhaps even at each other. You can produce uniformity by pressure from without, but unity comes only from power from within. Churches experience unity as they share Christ's life, while cults promote uniformity as they demand submission.

The church is more than an organization. It is an *organism*, a living body, energized by the Spirit of God. This is not to suggest that church organization is wrong, because if an organism is not organized, it will die. But when organization becomes more important than spiritual relationship to Christ, then "institutionalism" sets in and the church starts to exist only for itself. How tragic!

Local evangelical churches may differ from one another in minor matters of interpretation and organization, but it is important that they present to the world a united witness of love (John 13:34-35; 17:20-23). Why? Because God put the church into the world to help him "put things together." The Father's ultimate goal is that "he might gather together in one all things in Christ" (Eph. 1:10). If the local church is divided, and the divisions are competing with each other, then the church is working against the very plan of God.

As we read through Paul's letter to the Ephesians, we see the emphasis on "gathering all things together in Christ." In 2:1-10, God brings lost sinners back into fellowship with himself. In 2:11-22, believing Jews and Gentiles are made one in Christ. The unity of the whole church is emphasized doctrinally in 4:1-16 and practically in 4:17–5:17. The letter closes by emphasizing unity between husbands and wives (5:18-33), parents and children (6:1-4), and masters and servants (6:5-9). This unity on earth is accomplished through the church by the Head of the church in heaven. We are in this world to do the will of God and help "gather together all things in Christ." Ours is the "ministry of reconciliation" (2 Cor. 5:18-21).

The spiritual unity of God's people is not something that we must bring about ourselves. It is already an accomplished fact. "There is one body" (Eph. 4:4), not "There ought to be one body." Paul was not referring to some all-inclusive organization, a "world church," so to speak, but to the body of Jesus Christ in the world, a spiritual body made up of living members, people who have trusted Christ and received new life through the Spirit.

Here, then, is our second responsibility, to be enthusiastic to maintain and promote the spiritual unity of God's people. Be a peacemaker, not a troublemaker, and help to put things together in your world.

3. Diversity

You will note that all three of the important "body passages" in the New Testament deal with both unity and diversity:

Unity	Diversity
Rom. 12:1-5	Rom. 12:5-8
1 Cor. 12:1-13	1 Cor. 12:14-31
Eph. 4:1-6	Eph. 4:7-13

Unity and diversity must work together or one will destroy the other. Unity without diversity is uniformity, but diversity without unity is anarchy. The church needs *both* unity and diversity if it is to function in this world. God has given diverse gifts to his people and these gifts must be used for the building up of the body of Christ. We shall discover as we continue our study that the only thing that can balance unity and diversity is *maturity*, "growing up" to become more like Jesus Christ.

The various images of the church given in Ephesians illustrate this fine balance between unity and diversity. In 1:22-23 and 2:16 Paul used the human body as his example. I have one body, but it is made up of many different parts, each of which has an important function to perform. In 1 Corinthians 12:14-31 Paul amplifies this truth and points out that, in the body of Christ, Christians belong to each other, affect each other, and need each other.

In Ephesians 2:19 Paul used the *nation* and the *family* to illustrate unity and diversity. In a nation, there are many different kinds of people, but they are all citizens of one "body politic" and all have a part to play. Children in a family are all different, and yet they share the same parents and the same nature. You find in the nation and in the family both unity and diversity.

The building (2:20-22) is another illustration of unity (one plan) in diversity (many parts). Marriage (5:22ff.) also pictures this balance, for the husband and wife are different from each other and yet "one flesh." Finally, in 6:10ff., Paul wrote about the army and the spiritual armor. There is one army but it is made up of many individual soldiers, units, and companies. There must be unity (one loyalty, one commander, one enemy) and diversity (infantry, cavalry, intelligence, etc.). Of all these illustrations, perhaps the body is the clearest.

When the Holy Spirit baptizes the believer into the body of Christ at conversion, he gives that believer a spiritual gift, or spiritual gifts. The member of the body is to use the gift (or gifts) to help the body grow and mature (Eph. 4:7-16 and 1 Cor. 12:12-31). The church does not grow as the result of people using their special "talents" or abilities in their own strength. The church grows when gifted people use their gifts in the power of the Spirit.

Unity has to do with the *gift* of the Spirit, while diversity has to do with the *gifts* of the Spirit. But this is not enough: we must also have the *graces* of the Spirit if we are to use our gifts in the right way to the glory of God. It was here that the Corinthian church failed. They used their gifts as weapons to fight with, not as tools to build with, because they lacked love.

This leads to our fourth theme, *maturity*. But first, we had better mention our third responsibility, which is to discover and develop our own spiritual gifts and not be afraid of diversity in the church. When the Spirit is in control, diversity strengthens the vitality of the body by testing the unity of the body.

4. Maturity

Again, each of the "body passages" deals with maturity, which is expressed by Christian love. Now we are dealing with the *graces* of the Spirit, those beautiful qualities that the Spirit of God produces in our lives when we are functioning in the body as we should. Here is the complete chart of the "body passages":

Unity	Rom. 12:1-5	1 Cor. 12:1-13	Eph. 4:1-6
Diversity	Rom. 12:6-8	1 Cor. 12:14-31	Eph. 4:7-12
Maturity	Rom. 12:19-21	1 Cor. 13–14	Eph. 4:13-16
	[love]	[love]	[love]

First Corinthians 13 emphasizes love and 1 Corinthians 14 shows how that love should be exercised in the practical activities of the church. It is too bad that we think of 1 Corinthians 13 only as a lovely poem to be read at funerals and weddings, when actually it ought to be read at church business meetings. The Corinthian church was a needy assembly. It was divided (1:10-12); defiled (5:1ff.); and disgraced (6:1-8). In the public meetings, some of the "gifted members" were flaunting their gifts and causing disorder (11:17-18; 14:23-26). The more spectacular gifts, such as tongues, were especially being abused in the assembly.

How did Paul seek to correct this ugly situation? By

teaching them the truth about spiritual gifts. Each believer has at least one gift, and that gift must be used for the good of the whole church. The purpose of ministry is the building up of the body, not the promoting of the individual believer. Seven times in 1 Corinthians 14, Paul uses the word *edify* ("build up"). In the public meetings, there must always be edification, decency, and order (14:40).

The body matures from within. It must be nurtured with the Word as each member ministers (Eph. 4:11-12, 16). "Speaking the truth in love" is the secret of maturity (Eph. 4:15). It has well been said that truth without love is brutality, but love without truth is hypocrisy. We need both love and truth if the body is to mature and become more like Jesus Christ. The goal of our ministry is to grow "unto the measure of the stature of the fulness of Christ" (Eph. 4:13). God wants his people individually, and his church collectively, to become more and more like his Son (Rom. 8:29).

Of course, our glorified Head, Jesus Christ, is constantly ministering to his body through the Holy Spirit of God. This is the work our Lord is now doing in heaven. As each member of the body yields to Christ and permits the Spirit to minister, the body grows and is strengthened. Hebrews 13:21 informs us that Christ's desire is to "equip you with everything good for doing his will, and . . . work in us what is pleasing to him" (NIV).

The key word here is "equip," a translation of the Greek word *katartizo*. As we have seen, it means "to adjust, to equip, to prepare." Doctors used this word to describe the setting of a broken bone. To sailors it meant the outfitting of a ship for a voyage; and to soldiers it meant the equipping of an army for battle. Fishermen used it to describe the mending of their nets (see Matt. 4:21).

What, then, is Jesus Christ now doing for the members of his body? He is adjusting and setting the "broken bones" so that the body will be strong and healthy. He is equipping us for the voyages and the battles of life, and he

is "repairing us" so that we can be effective tools in his
hands.

But, how does he do this? If you trace *katartizo* and its
kindred words through the New Testament, you will see
that our Lord uses four special tools to equip us for ministry in the body.

First, he uses *the Word of God.* "All Scripture is God-
breathed and is useful for teaching, rebuking, correcting
and training in righteousness, so that the man of God may
be thoroughly equipped *[exartizo]* for every good work"
(2 Tim. 3:16-17, NIV). The believer who reads and studies
the Bible, who meditates on it and seeks to obey its truths,
will find himself growing and being useful to Christ and
his church.

I have watched this process in my years of ministry, and
it has never ceased to excite me. You lead people to faith in
Christ and then introduce them to serious Bible study. At
first, the new Christians flounder a bit ("Where did you
say Genesis was?"), but then things start to fall into place.
The "babes" begin to grow, and along with growth comes
a desire to serve. Then you discover how the Word has
helped them discover and develop spiritual gifts that can
be used to build up the church. What a thrill!

The second tool our Lord uses is *the fellowship of the local church.* "It was he who gave some to be apostles, some
to be prophets, some to be evangelists, and some to be pastors and teachers, to prepare [*katartizo*] God's people for
works of service, so that the body of Christ may be built
up" (Eph. 4:11-12, NIV).

The sequence here is clear. God provides gifted leaders
to the church, and these leaders help the believers discover
and develop their own spiritual gifts. As each believer ministers to the body, the body grows and more leaders are de-
veloped in the church to help the next generation.
Christians who ignore the local fellowship of believers are
missing opportunities for growth. Radio, television, books,
tapes, and seminars all have their place and can be used

of God. But there is no substitute for the local church when it comes to balanced spiritual growth.

Then why today does there appear to be a shortage of *spiritual* officers, teachers, pastors, and Christian workers? Because far too many churches "hire" gifted people to do the work that the individual members ought to be doing, instead of encouraging these leaders to equip the church through the Word. Vance Havner said, "I have seen good men become the flunkies and bellhops of their congregation." That is not the way God meant it to be.

The first internal crisis the early church faced had to do with the priorities of their spiritual leaders (Acts 6:1-7). The problem was solved when the church agreed to change the organization and share some of the responsibility and authority so that the apostles could major on "prayer and the ministry of the word" (Acts 6:4). The result? "So the word of God spread. The number of disciples in Jerusalem increased rapidly" (Acts 6:7, NIV).

To quote Vance Havner again: "Many a man called to be a preacher wears out in trivial missions, not necessarily evil, but not worth his time and effort. It is important to get our priorities in place."

Another part of the local church's "equipping" ministry is the loving discipline and restoration of erring members. "Brothers, if someone is caught in a sin, you who are spiritual should restore him gently. But watch yourself, or you also may be tempted" (Gal. 6:1, NIV). A believer who is out of fellowship with God and the church is like a bone out of joint or broken. It must be set with tenderness and patience or else the whole body will be infected and weakened.

The third spiritual "tool" that the risen Savior uses to equip his people is *prayer*. "Our prayer is for your perfection" [*katartizo*] (2 Cor. 13:9, NIV), Paul wrote. Prayer releases the power of God in our lives and in the lives of others, and this leads to spiritual growth and service.

What a blessing, and yet what a battle, it is to pray for

God's people and watch them develop and start to serve Jesus Christ! No doubt Paul was thrilled as he saw the Lord equip Timothy and Titus for ministry. Often in his work Paul had to leave young churches behind, and all he could do was pray for the leaders and write them letters of encouragement. When he visited those churches months later, he rejoiced to see how God had matured and equipped some of his people.

The fourth tool God uses to equip his own is *suffering for the sake of Jesus Christ.* "And the God of all grace, who called you to his eternal glory in Christ, after you have suffered a little while, will himself restore you [*katartizo*] and make you strong, firm and steadfast" (1 Pet. 5:10, NIV).

In his first letter, Peter had a great deal to say about the sufferings of God's people. Some of his readers were burdened because of the trials of life (1:6-7). Others were being lied about (2:12), and some of the believers were suffering because they had done good, not evil (2:18-20; 3:13-14, 17). Peter told them that a "fiery trial" would soon begin and that they would suffer because they bore the name of Jesus Christ (4:12-19).

Satan wants to use suffering to tear us down, but God can use suffering to build us up and equip us to serve him better. However, keep in mind that suffering does not *automatically* equip the saint. Sad to say, some Christians have gone through trials and have come out of the fiery furnace burned and bitter instead of purified and perfected. It is only when we depend on the grace of "the God of all grace" that the furnace does its equipping work.

Here is our fourth responsibility: we must let God use his "tools" to equip us and mature us as we share in the ministry of the local church. We must devote quality time to the Word of God, prayer, Christian fellowship, and worship, and we must not be afraid of the furnaces. The Head of the church in heaven knows exactly what to do to help us mature.

5. Ministry

We have considered four words that help us understand what it means for the Christian to be a member of Christ's body: vitality, unity, diversity, and maturity. One word remains: ministry.

When the Son of God came to earth to minister, he needed a physical body (Heb. 10:5-7). When he returned to heaven after his earthly work was completed, he left behind a spiritual body, the church. The birth of his physical body is recorded in Luke 2, and the birth of his spiritual body in Acts 2, both written by Dr. Luke.

Why is his spiritual body here on earth? To continue his work and to share his message with the whole world. A body is for ministry.

In recent years "body life" has captured the interest of many churches. In some places it has almost become a fad. During the sixties I heard the question, "What is your gift, brother?" so many times that I felt like hanging a sign around my neck that read: "It may not look like it, but I think I have the gift of teaching the Word and shepherding the flock." However, I couldn't find a saint with the gift of sign-painting!

When "body life" really catches on, the local church starts to minister in new and exciting ways that are sometimes difficult to keep up with. People discover that there are other kinds of Christian service beside preaching, teaching, singing, taking up the collection, visiting prospects, and sitting on committees. Not that these tasks are unimportant; but if this is *all* that the church does, then a lot of people are spectators instead of participants. D. L. Moody once said, "I would rather put ten men to work than do the work of ten men." That is what "body life" is all about. It means equipping God's people, enlisting them for service, and then encouraging them to get the job done. Booker T. Washington said, "Few things help an individual more than to place a responsibility upon him, and let him know that you trust him."

We speak about "church membership" as though it were only a matter of "joining church" and "supporting" the church with our money, attendance, and occasional work. But "membership" means that we are part of a living body and have the responsibility and privilege of contributing to the strength and growth of that body. If the body is to grow and serve, it must be "joined and held together by *every* supporting ligament . . . as *each* part does its work" (Eph. 4:16, NIV; italics mine).

Now we are ready for our fifth responsibility: we must use our gift(s) in loving ministry *to* the church and *through* the church to a needy world. We must do the thing God has called us to do, and do it in his power and for his glory.

As we take time to review the five key words and the five responsibilities we have as Christians, we should rejoice at what an exciting thing it is to be a member of the body of Christ!

CHAPTER 5

A Priest at God's Altar

God's purpose for the nation of Israel was that they be a "kingdom of priests and a holy nation" (Exod. 19:6), but they failed God and lost their spiritual privileges. Those privileges are now enjoyed by the church, for the New Testament says that we are "a holy priesthood . . . a chosen generation, a royal priesthood, an holy nation . . . " and "a kingdom of priests" (1 Pet. 2:5, 9; Rev. 1:6).

Under the old covenant, God's people *had* a priesthood; but in the new covenant, God's people *are* a priesthood. "The priesthood of the believer" is a precious article of the Christian faith, the defense of which has cost many a life. It means that all believers have the same acceptance before God and enjoy equal access to God through Jesus Christ, the Great High Priest.

"Therefore all Christians are priests," said Martin Luther, "and accursed be the statement that a priest is something different from a Christian." In fact, Luther, like most of the Reformers, disapproved when people called the ministers of the church "priests." He made it clear that "those who serve people with the Word and Sacraments may and must not be called priests. . . . According to the evangelical writings [the New Testament epistles] they

should be called ministers, deacons, bishops and stewards."

His point is simply that *all believers are priests*, and no
Christian should allow any other Christian to come between him and his Lord. All Christians are invited to come
boldly into God's presence to worship him and present
their needs (Heb. 4:14-16; 10:19-22). Jesus Christ today is
our High Priest in heaven, and there he represents us and
intercedes for us before the Father (Heb. 8:1ff.).

1. The Process: Becoming a Priest (Exod. 29).

How does a person become one of God's priests? The "process" is illustrated in the Old Testament ceremony of the
induction of Aaron and his sons into the priesthood. Notice
the steps that were involved and how they illustrate the
New Testament priesthood.

They were chosen and called by God (29:1-4). Every Jew
in the camp did not become a priest, but only those chosen
by God—Aaron and his sons. In order to become a priest
one had to be born into the right family. And that is exactly the way we become a New Testament priest, by being
born into God's family (John 1:12-13; 3:1-16). It was not a
matter of education, ability, or achievement. Perhaps there
were others in Israel who were smarter, more skillful, and
more personable than Aaron and his sons. But it made no
difference. God had chosen Aaron and that settled it.

All Christians are chosen and called by God (Eph. 1:4;
2 Thess. 2:13-14; John 15:16). They have nothing in themselves that merits God's salvation. It is wholly of grace
(Eph. 2:8-10). No stranger in the camp of Israel was permitted even to come near to the priestly ministry on penal-
ty of death (Num. 3:10).

They were washed (29:4). This was a bathing of the
whole person, and it symbolized the cleansing of their
sins. The priests were to represent the people before God,

and this meant maintaining a holy life (Zech. 3). As Christian priests, we have also been washed, and therefore we stand cleansed before God. "Unto him that loved us, and washed us from our sins in his own blood, and hath made us kings and priests unto God" (Rev. 1:5-6).

No matter how sinful we may have been, God washed us when we trusted his Son as our Savior (1 Cor. 6:9-11). We must not equate this washing with baptism, because baptism does not wash away our sins (1 Pet. 3:21). It is "the washing of regeneration [the new birth], and renewing of the Holy Spirit" that accomplishes the cleansing of the sinful heart (Titus 3:5). God purifies our hearts by faith (Acts 15:9), not by means of religious ceremonies. Baptism is an important witness of our salvation (Acts 10:47-48), but it is not the means of our salvation.

It is important to note that a bullock and two rams were slain as sacrifices for Aaron and his sons (29:10-25). It is a biblical principle that "without shedding of blood is no remission" (Heb. 9:22; Lev. 17:11). We have been cleansed, not by the blood of animal sacrifices, but by the precious blood of Jesus (Heb. 9:11-15).

The blood of the sacrifice was applied to the right ear, right thumb, and right big toe of Aaron and his sons (29:19-20). This was a reminder that they were to consecrate their whole body to the work of the Lord (Rom. 12:1), listen to his Word, do his work, and walk in his ways.

They were clothed (29:5-9). God told Moses to have special garments made for Aaron and his sons (Exod. 28). Unless they were properly attired, they could not minister in the tabernacle. And if they did minister without wearing these garments, it could cost them their lives (Exod. 28:43).

Ever since Adam and Eve sinned, man's nakedness has been a problem to him. Man tried to cover his nakedness, first by hiding from God, and then by wearing fig leaves

(Gen. 3:10-11). God in his grace shed blood and clothed Adam and Eve (Gen. 3:21), a picture of what he did for us when Jesus died on the cross. Jesus was made sin for us so that we might wear the robe of his righteousness and stand "accepted in the beloved" (2 Cor. 5:21; Isa. 61:10; Eph. 1:6).

They were anointed (29:7). This anointing oil was very special because it was prescribed by God and could be used only for holy purposes (Exod. 30:22-33). It is a symbol of the Holy Spirit of God who has anointed every believer (2 Cor. 1:21; 1 John 2:27; and note Acts 10:38). It is not necessary for Christians to pray for the anointing of the Spirit because every believer has already been anointed. What we need to do is believe the Word and permit the Spirit to work in our lives.

They were satisfied (29:22-37). Moses gave the priests part of the "ram of consecration" as their food. The priests were given stated portions from some of the sacrifices as their remuneration for service. A faithful priest would never go hungry! (In fact, one of them overdid it; see 1 Sam. 4:18.) The spiritual lesson is clear: as we serve the Lord, he supplies our needs and satisfies us.

As a "holy priesthood" (1 Pet. 2:5), we are set apart for God's exclusive service. As a "royal priesthood" (1 Pet. 2:9), we share our Lord's authority, for he is both King and Priest. Jesus is not a priest after the order of Aaron, because Aaron served on earth and Jesus serves in heaven. According to Hebrews 7–9, our Lord's priesthood is "after the order of Melchisedek" who was *both* a king and a priest (Gen. 14:17-24; Heb. 7:1-11). No king in Israel was permitted to serve as priest, and no priest ruled as a king. Jesus Christ alone unites all three of the Old Testament offices; he is prophet, priest, and king.

Let us pause to thank God that we are saved and have been made into a kingdom of priests! In fact, as we consider the privileges of the priesthood, we ought to praise him even more!

2. The Privileges: Ministering as a Priest

Aaron and his sons, and their descendants, enjoyed some special privileges that were forbidden to other people in the nation of Israel. Each of these privileges applies in a spiritual way to the New Testament believer in the church today.

Caring for God's dwelling place (Num. 3). The three families of tribe of Levi were put in complete charge of the tabernacle, with each family assigned a specific area of ministry. The Gershonites cared for the tabernacle coverings and hangings; the Kohathites were in charge of the furniture and vessels; and the families of Merari supervised the tabernacle structure, the boards, bars, pillars, and other equipment. It was all carefully organized because this was God's dwelling, and everything had to be done decently and in order (1 Cor. 14:40).

What is God's dwelling place on earth today? The individual believer (1 Cor. 6:19-20), the local church (1 Cor. 3:16-17, and note the plural pronouns), and the whole church collectively (Eph. 2:20-22). In general, we can say that in this present age, God dwells *in* his people and not simply *among* them (Exod. 25:8). Under the old covenant, God's people *made him* a sanctuary. But under the new covenant, God's people *are* his sanctuary.

This means that we as believer-priests have the wonderful privilege of caring for God's dwelling place. This begins with the care of our own bodies, which are the temple of God. A Christian should no more defile his body than a Jew would defile the temple or the tabernacle. Caring for one's body is much more than showing good sense or even practicing good health. It is an act of worship and service to the Lord who lives within (Rom. 12:1-2).

Those who make a distinction in the Christian life between the "spiritual" and the "physical" are making a false distinction. God wants the whole person to be holy—spirit, soul, and body (1 Thess. 5:23). Can you imagine a husband saying to his wife, "I will love you with my mind and heart, but what I do with my body is my business"? There would not be much of a future for that marriage!

God also wants the local assembly of believers to be a holy temple for his glory (1 Cor. 3:16-17). It is tragic to see some professed Christians defile the local church by their sinful actions and attitudes. Then they get angry and leave and start attending another church. Before long, they are causing trouble there and the cycle is repeated. "If any man defile the temple of God, him shall God destroy" (1 Cor. 3:17). *Defile* and *destroy* are translations of the same Greek word, which means "to defile, to destroy, to corrupt." God will deal with those who defile and destroy the purity and ministry of the local church. We must care for God's dwelling place because we are his priests.

Keeping the fire burning (Lev. 6:12-13). When Moses and Aaron dedicated the tabernacle, fire came from God and consumed the sacrifices on the brazen altar (Lev. 9:22-24). It was the responsibility of the priests each morning to remove the old ashes, put on fresh wood, and keep the fire burning. Without the fire on the altar, the people could not offer their sacrifices to God.

All of this has a spiritual application to us as believers, for each of us has a "spiritual temperature." God wants us to have burning hearts (Luke 24:32), but too often we are lukewarm (Rev. 3:16) or even cold (Matt. 24:12). Paul admonished Timothy to "stir up the gift of God" (2 Tim. 1:6), which literally means "put life into the fire again." The New International Version reads "fan into full flame," and *The Living Bible* says "stir into flame."

It is our responsibility to keep the fire burning brightly on the altar of our heart. We must get rid of the old ashes from past sacrifices and blessings, add fresh fuel each morning, and ask the Spirit of God—the breath of God—to blow upon the fire and bring it into a blaze to the glory of God. Neglect will always hurt the fire (1 Tim. 4:14), and when the fire gets low, then we become lukewarm Christians, or even cold Christians.

Washing at the laver (Exod. 30:17-21). As the priests served God in the tabernacle or temple, their hands and feet got dirty. God commanded them to wash their hands and feet at the brass laver in the holy place. And if they did not wash, they were in danger of death. This same principle applies to God's believer-priests today: if we want to have fellowship with the Lord, we must come to him for cleansing (John 13:1-11; 1 John 1:5–2:2). The priests were *washed all over* at their initial ordination, which is a picture of salvation. But they needed this regular cleansing, which is a picture of daily sanctification.

Burning the incense (Exod. 30:7-9). There were two altars in God's sanctuary, a brazen altar that stood at the door and was used for the blood sacrifices, and a golden altar that stood before the veil and was used for the burning of incense. The golden altar pictures the offering up of prayer to the Lord (Ps. 141:1-3; Luke 1:5-17). What a privilege it is to pray to the Father! Believers in this present age have an even greater privilege than did the priests, for we are invited to come boldly into the very presence of God and give our petitions to him (Heb. 10:19-25). When Jesus died on the cross, the veil of the temple was torn in two, for he opened up the new and living way.

As the priest burned the incense each morning and evening, some of its fragrance would cling to him, and people would know that he had been at the golden altar. As we pray, there should be a spiritual fragrance in our lives that lets others know we have been with Jesus. "We are all priests," said Martin Luther, "and our praying is the burning of incense."

Lighting the lamps (Exod. 30:7-8). The seven-branched golden candlestick stood before the veil to the right of the golden altar. It was the priest's responsibility to trim the wicks each morning and light the lamps each evening. This candlestick primarily spoke of God's light and truth shining through the nation of Israel to a dark and sinful world. It can be applied to the testimony of the church

(Rev. 1:9-20) as well as to the witness of the individual believer (Matt. 5:14-16). Some students believe that the lamp is a symbol of God's Word (Ps. 119:105; 2 Pet. 1:19).

The priest attended to the lamp in connection with his ministry at the altar of incense because prayer and witness go together (Acts 4:31), as do prayer and the Word of God (Acts 6:4).

Eating the bread (Exod. 25:23-30; Lev. 24:5-9). Each Sabbath, the priest placed twelve loaves of special bread on the table in the holy place, and only the priests were permitted to eat it. The loaves reminded the priests that their nourishment (physical and spiritual) came from God. Jesus Christ is the "bread of life" (John 6:33ff.); he, like the manna, was sent down from heaven to give spiritual life to the world. But he is also the "showbread" in the sanctuary, given to sustain life. We must feed on Christ if we are to have the spiritual strength we need for our pilgrim journey.

Entering through the veil (Lev. 16). When the priest got to the veil that separated the holy place from the holy of holies, he had to stop. Only once a year, on the Day of Atonement, was the high priest allowed to go past the veil and into the presence of the glory of God. But the believer-priest today can enter God's presence at any time because the way has been opened by Jesus Christ (Heb. 10:19-25). In fact, the believer-priest has the privilege of *living* "within the veil" at all times.

It is important that we see the beautiful sequence that is illustrated by the tabernacle. We start at the brazen altar where the blood is shed for our cleansing. Then we enter the holy place where we cleanse our hands and feet before we approach the golden altar of prayer. We feed on the bread and trim the lamp, but we don't stop there. The veil has been opened and we can go into the holy of holies, into the very presence of God.

What was in the holy of holies? The Ark of the Covenant was there, symbolizing the throne of God (Exod. 25:10-22; Pss. 80:1; 99:1). The golden mercy seat with the cherubim sat on the Ark, and the glory of God filled the holy of holies. God reigned from this "throne of grace" (Heb. 4:14-16) and communed with his people. Each year, on the Day of Atonement, the high priest sprinkled blood on the mercy seat and covered the sins of Israel. When Jesus died, his blood *took away* the sins of the world (John 1:29).

The three general themes of Hebrews are: (1) "Let us go on" (spiritual maturity, 6:1), (2) "Let us go in" (fellowship with God, 10:19ff.), and (3) "Let us go out" (identification with Christ in his rejection, 13:13). It takes all three for a balanced life.

Offering the spiritual sacrifices (1 Pet. 2:5). As God's priests, we bring "spiritual sacrifices" to him through Jesus Christ who is our "altar" (Heb. 13:10). The word *spiritual* does not suggest "immaterial," because some of the sacrifices we give are definitely material. Rather, *spiritual* means "of a spiritual quality." If unsaved people offered them, these sacrifices would not be spiritual, nor would they be accepted by God.

We have already noted that *prayer* is a sacrifice we offer to the Lord (Ps. 141:1-3), and so is our *praise of God* (Heb. 13:15). God sees our *good works* as spiritual sacrifices (Heb. 13:16), as well as the *money* we give for his service (Phil. 4:14-18; Rom. 15:27). God certainly wants *our bodies* yielded to him as a living sacrifice, not a dead one (Rom. 12:1-2); and he also wants us to give him our hearts (Ps. 51:17).

The winning of others to Christ is also an act of spiritual worship (Rom. 15:16). The words *minister* and *ministering* come from a Greek word that means "priestly service" and gives us our English word *liturgy.* Paul looked upon the Gentile converts as a sacrifice "offered up" to the Lord (Eph. 5:2; Heb. 10:5, 8). This lifts evangelism to the highest plane possible, for when we witness to others and win them to Christ, we are performing acts of worship to the Lord. Witnessing is not "Christian salesmanship." It is a holy act of worship to the glory of God.

3. The Perils: Defiling the Priesthood (Mal. 1:6–2:9)
Wherever there are privileges there are also perils, and no
book in the Bible spells out the perils of the priesthood
more vividly than Malachi (note 1:6; 2:1, 7). What sins
were the priests committing as they carried on their duties
in the restored temple?

To begin with, they were dishonoring God by defiling
his name (1:6). How? By not giving their best on the altar.
They offered polluted bread and imperfect sacrifices and
kept the best for themselves. Malachi used a bit of sancti-
fied sarcasm when he said, "Offer these same sick and
handicapped animals as a gift to your governor, and see if
he will accept them!" When we fail to give our best to
God, we defile the priesthood.

The work they were doing was useless; no spiritual
benefits came from their services (1:10). It would have
been better had somebody shut the gates of the temple and
put out the fire on the altar! Why? Because no good was
accomplished by their ministry. (See Isaiah 1:10-15.) The
priests were listlessly going through the motions, saying,
"What a weariness is it!" (1:13). Better that they were either hot or cold, and not lukewarm (Rev. 3:16)!

The greatest tragedy was that they were robbing God of
his glory (2:1-2; see 1 Pet. 2:9). Their hypocritical ministry
was a terrible testimony to the godless nations around
them, people who desperately needed to know about the
true and living God.

What did God do because of their sins? He cursed their
blessings (2:2-3). He didn't take their blessings away. He
simply transformed their blessings into curses. What
should have brought joy to them and their nation was instead the channel of sorrow. After the temple services, the
people returned home in worse spiritual condition than if
they had not participated at all. Instead of carrying away
the fragrance of God's blessing, they smelled like dung
(2:3; compare John 12:1-8). Alas, instead of guiding peo-

ple into the right way, the priests were causing them to stumble (2:4-9).

This is not a very pretty picture, but neither is it an ancient picture. These same sins are with us today. Review the privileges you have as a believer-priest, and honestly ask yourself, "Am I using these privileges for God's glory? Am I giving my best on the altar?" Perhaps one reason the church has such a weak witness in today's world is because we as priests have forfeited our privileges and are living on substitutes; and God is cursing our blessings.

Is there hope? Yes, there is always hope. If we confess our sins and admit our need, the Great High Priest will cleanse us and restore our spiritual blessings.

"For he will sit as a refiner and purifier of silver; he will purify the Levites and refine them like gold and silver. Then the LORD will have men who will bring offerings in righteousness" (Mal. 3:3, NIV).

At the turn of the century, Dr. G. Campbell Morgan gave a series of messages at Moody's Northfield Conference on the subject of the Minor Prophets. In his message on Malachi, Dr. Morgan said that "the vast bulk of Christendom has become characterized by ritual rather than by life, by form without power. Was there ever such a day of machinery as this? Was the church of God ever so packed full in every corner with machines, machines, wheels, wheels, organizations, organizations? Yet in spite of all this machinery and activity, the heathen world is still gaining on us by leaps and bounds" (*The Minor Prophets*, Revell, 1960, 156).

Morgan should see the church today!

God is looking for holy priests who will offer up spiritual sacrifices that will glorify his name. Will you be one of them?

CHAPTER 6

A Stone in God's Building

Since it was Simon whom Jesus nick-named "Peter, a stone" (John 1:42), it is only fitting that he be selected by the Spirit to tell us about Christ the stone and how we as Christians are related to him. Peter wrote:

As you come to him, the living Stone—rejected by men but chosen by God and precious to him—you also, like living stones, are being built into a spiritual house to be a holy priesthood, offering spiritual sacrifices acceptable to God through Jesus Christ. For in Scripture it says: "See, I lay a stone in Zion, a chosen and precious cornerstone, and the one who trusts in him will never be put to shame." Now to you who believe, this stone is precious. But to those who do not believe, "The stone the builders rejected has become the capstone," and "A stone that causes men to stumble and a rock that makes them fall." They stumble because they disobey the message—which is also what they were destined for. (1 Pet. 2:4-8, NIV)

The emphasis is on Jesus Christ, and Peter presented him in three different portraits. Peter also explained how we as his people relate to him in these three portraits.

When we understand what we are in him, it can make a difference in our life, service, and worship.

1. Jesus Christ the Stone

The image of God as "Rock" was certainly familiar to the Jewish people. "He is the Rock, his work is perfect" (Deut. 32:4). "Unto thee will I cry, O Lord my rock" (Ps. 28:1). "He only is my rock and my salvation" (Ps. 62:2, 6). A rock reminds us of stability, security, and strength. "God is our refuge and strength, a very present help in trouble" (Ps. 46:1). So, when Peter called Jesus Christ the "living Stone," he was clearly affirming that Jesus Christ is God. That was Peter's own testimony of faith (Matt. 16:16; John 6:66-69).

What kind of a stone is Jesus Christ? To begin with, he is the *living Stone* (1 Pet. 2:4) because he is the living God. He died for us, was raised from the dead, and will live forever to share his life with us. We sometimes say that something is "as dead as a rock" or "stone dead," but you could never say that related to Jesus. Because we have trusted the living Stone (2:4), we have been born again to a living hope (1:3) through the living Word of God (1:22-23). There was a time when we were lost sinners, "stone dead" in the pit of sin; but Jesus Christ has lifted us up and given us life. We are now living stones.

He is also the *chief cornerstone* (1 Pet. 2:6-7). We today usually think of the cornerstone as something decorative but not too important to the actual structure. We engrave on it the name of the building, the date when the stone was laid, and whatever other data the building committee thinks is important for future generations to know. In Bible times the cornerstone was not looked upon as a decoration. It could be the stone that tied the two walls together at the corner, or the capstone that completed the building, or perhaps the keystone of the arch. In any case, this stone was definitely important.

As chief cornerstone, Jesus Christ unites all that God is doing to bring things together in this world. He is the "living link" between the Old Testament and the New Testament (Luke 24:25-27). He binds together in the church Jews and Gentiles who have trusted him (Eph. 2:11-22). If the cornerstone is wrong, then the whole building will be wrong, and God's purposes will not be fulfilled. But the cornerstone is right and will be forever.

He is a *chosen (elect) Stone* (2:4, 6). This means not only "selected" but also "select, special." Jesus Christ is unique, and no one else can be compared with him. No one can take his place. He has been chosen by the Father, and that is recommendation enough for me.

After speaking at a booksellers' convention in California, I was greeting people when a young lady approached who said she had a very special message for me: she had met Jesus Christ on the beach that morning! She then introduced me to a seedy looking character with long dirty hair and beard to match. I reached out and took one of his hands. "There are no nail prints here," I said, "so you are not Jesus Christ. You are a phony." The very idea of some beach bum claiming to be God's elect Stone!

To the Father, the Stone is *precious* (2:4, 6). "This is my beloved Son, in whom I am well pleased" (Matt. 3:17). According to Peter, everything about Jesus Christ is precious: precious blood (1:19), precious faith (2 Pet. 1:1), and precious promises (2 Pet. 1:4). Even the trials we endure are precious for his sake (1 Pet. 1:7). The better we get to know him, the more precious he becomes in our lives.

The word translated "precious" carries with it the idea of honor as well as value. To us who know and love him, Jesus Christ is worthy of all honor (Rev. 5:12-14). The religious leaders in Jesus' day rejected him as a deceiver and a troublemaker. As far as they were concerned, he was worthy of only one thing—death. When they crucified him, he became the *smitten Stone* that provides the water of life to thirsty sinners (Exod. 17:1-7; 1 Cor. 10:4; John 7:37-39). In his two epistles, Peter has a good deal to say about the death of Jesus Christ and what it has accomplished for us.

He is a *dependable stone*: "the one who trusts in him will never be put to shame" (1 Pet. 2:6, NIV, quoted from Isa. 28:16). The Greek text uses a double negative: "He shall not, no never, be ashamed." Kenneth Wuest translated it: "He shall never be defeated." We can depend on Jesus Christ; faith in him will never lead to disappointment. After all, faith is only as good as its object. If we trust money, we get what money can do. Trust ourselves and we get what we can do. Trust Jesus Christ and we get what God can do! "Confidence in the natural world is self-reliance," wrote Oswald Chambers; "in the spiritual world it is God-reliance."

To God the Father, Jesus Christ is chosen and precious; and to us as believers, he is precious and dependable. But what is he to the unbelieving world? He is the *rejected Stone* that causes offense and stumbling (2:4, 7-8). The "religious experts" in Israel did not even recognize their own Messiah and ended up rejecting the most important stone in God's building. This tragic deed was predicted by God the Father (Ps. 118:22-23) and preached by God the Son (Matt. 21:42-46). Through the Apostle Peter, God the Spirit rebuked the "religious experts" for their blindness (Acts 4:11). Alas, far too many religious "experts" are just as blind today.

Why did the "experts" reject him? Because they disobeyed the Word and stumbled over it (see Isa. 8:14-15). They were anticipating a royal Messiah who would defeat Rome and establish David's great kingdom once again. Instead, they were confronted by a humble servant who suffered and died. (See Rom. 9:30-33 and 1 Cor. 1:18-23 for Paul's explanation of Jewish unbelief.) "They stumble, being disobedient to the word" (1 Pet. 2:8, NKJV). The word *disobey* means "not able to be persuaded." They had their own traditional interpretations of God's Word and they would not even consider the possibility that they might be wrong.

What will happen to those who reject God's elect Stone? They will be judged by the *smiting Stone*. "Whoever falls on this stone will be broken," said Jesus, "but on whomever it falls, it will grind him to powder" (Matt. 21:44). This judgment applies nationally as well as individually. One day Jesus shall return in power, judge the nations, and then establish his own glorious kingdom on the earth (Dan. 2:34-35, 44-45).

2. Jesus Christ the Builder

When our Lord was growing up in Nazareth, he worked with Joseph as a carpenter (Matt. 13:55; Mark 6:3). In that day a carpenter not only made plows, tools, and furniture, but he also helped to construct buildings. Jesus was a builder, and he is still a builder. In heaven he is building his people a home (John 14:1-6), and on earth he is building himself a church (Matt. 16:18). Saved people are the "living stones" that are being built into God's "spiritual house." We are being "built together to become a dwelling in which God lives by his Spirit" (Eph. 2:22).

Throughout the ages, God has had many different dwelling places. During the time of the Patriarchs, God walked with men as they obeyed and trusted him. Enoch walked with God (Gen. 5:24), as did Noah (Gen. 6:9) and Abraham (Gen. 17:1; 24:40). After Israel was delivered from Egypt, God instructed Moses to build him a house so that he might dwell with his people (Exod. 25:8). When Moses dedicated the house, the glory of God moved in (Exod. 40:34). Solomon built him a temple, and again God's glory came to dwell there (1 Kings 8:10-11). But Israel sinned and God had to remove his glory from the temple (Ezek. 8:4; 9:3; 10:4, 22-23). He then permitted the Babylonians to destroy both Jerusalem and the temple.

The next earthly dwelling place for God's glory was the body of his Son, Jesus Christ. "And the Word was made flesh, and dwelt [tabernacled] among us, and we beheld his glory" (John 1:14). Sinners took that body and nailed it to a cross, but Jesus Christ arose from the dead and went back to heaven to share in the glory once again (John 17:5, 24). Today, God does not live in man-made temples (Acts 7:48-50). His temples are the individual believer (1 Cor. 6:19-20), the local assembly of saints (1 Cor. 3:16), and the church universal (Eph. 2:20-22).

Each Christian is a "living stone," placed into the temple as God sees fit. This temple is not yet completed; Jesus Christ is still building his church. Perhaps when Peter wrote those words he had Solomon's temple in mind. "And the king commanded them to quarry large stones, costly stones, and hewn stones, to lay the foundation of the temple. . . . And the temple, when it was being built, was built with stone finished at the quarry, so that no hammer or chisel or any iron tool was heard in the temple while it was being built" (1 Kings 5:17; 6:7, NKJV).

The only way Solomon's engineers could have accomplished this was by following a master plan. God gave that plan to David and he shared it with Solomon (1 Chron. 28:11-19). Because the workers followed God's plan, the temple was built without noise or confusion. Every stone was prepared and fitted into its rightful place.

God has a master plan for his church (Eph. 1:4-12). He is hewing stones out of the quarry of sin, giving them life, and fitting them into his temple. He alone sees the total plan, and he alone knows when the temple will be completed. When Solomon's temple was completed, God moved in. But when the church is completed, God will move it out and take it to glory.

It encourages me when I realize that there is a vast difference between the church God sees and the church I see. I can see only a small fraction of the total picture, but God sees it all. I wonder why some of the stones are placed where they are, but God knows why and he makes no mistakes. I sometimes think that God's work is moving very slowly and ought to be speeded up, but then I remember that a thousand years to him is like one day.

But then it encourages me when I remind myself that I am a living stone in his temple—what a privilege!—and that all he asks of me is that I faithfully fill my place of ministry. When a building stone gets out of place, it becomes a stumbling block. Some Christians take themselves too seriously. They think they are supporting the whole building. If each living stone submits to God's preparation and fills the place of God's choosing, then the temple will continue to grow and become beautiful in the Lord.

A friend was encouraging me to pray for a mutual acquaintance who was starting to show symptoms of pride in his ministry. "He needs our help," said my friend. "Once a day he phones Dial-a-Prayer to see if there are any messages for him!" An exaggeration, of course, but it made his point eloquently.

Jesus Christ is not only building his church as a habitation of God, but he is also building the lives of his people. When Andrew brought his brother Simon to Jesus, he was no doubt surprised to hear the Master give Simon a new name —Peter (Greek), Cephas (Aramaic), both meaning "a stone" (John 1:42). At that point in his life, Simon was anything but a stone! But during the next three years, Jesus turned that piece of clay called Simon into Peter, the stone. It took some heat and some pressure, but he did it—and he didn't stop there. He turned that rock into a precious jewel (Rev. 21:14, 19).

The impatient, modern Christian wants instant spiritual maturity. After all, we get instant meals from our freezers and microwaves, instant data from our computers, and instant photographs from our cameras. Why not instant Christlikeness from our seminars? Because it takes time to turn clay into stone and stone into a precious jewel. You can manufacture artificial jewels in a special high compression machine, but you can't manufacture saints that way. It takes time to be holy. You can increase the speed of an automobile or an airplane, but you can't increase the speed of growing an oak or building a Christlike character.

Jesus Christ is the Master Builder. He is building his church and building the lives of his people. He is constantly cleansing and polishing his living stones to make them more useful and more beautiful. He is fitting us for ministry today and for service throughout all eternity.

3. Believers as Builders

As "living stones," believers have a relationship to one another as well as to Jesus Christ. He is not only the Builder, but he is also the foundation (1 Cor. 3:10-11) and the chief cornerstone of God's church, the temple that he is building for eternity (Eph. 2:20-22). He places each stone just where it ought to be. And if that stone is out of place, it may cause others to stumble.

But keep in mind that we are "*living* stones" and we have an influence on one another. The New Testament uses the word *edify* to describe this influence. It comes from the Latin word *edificio*, which means "to build." When Christians edify one another, they build up one another and make the church strong.

How can the "living stones" edify one another? Several personal admonitions from Paul, the master builder (1 Cor. 3:10), help to answer that question.

We help to build each other when we *practice love in all we do and say.* The Corinthian believers were very proud of their "knowledge" of spiritual things (1 Cor. 1:4-5), but they were using that knowledge to attack one another, not to help one another. How true it is that "knowledge puffs up" (1 Cor. 8:1). The believer who thinks he "knows it all" and monopolizes every Bible study discussion or committee meeting is only proving that he is proud and ignorant of his own basic need for Christian love.

Love "builds up" because love accepts others, even when there are disagreements. Love is patient and kind and creates an atmosphere in which people can understand each other and help each other. Love does not compete or compare. It seeks only to build people up and glorify the Lord.

We build others *by a godly example* (Rom. 14:1–15:4). The Roman assemblies were divided over how to practice the special diets and days given to the Jews in the Old Testament Law. The weaker saints, who may have been converted Jews, felt obligated to practice and defend the Law; but the stronger believers, who understood God's grace, wanted to practice their liberty in Christ. What a dilemma!

The answer? First, Paul admonished the stronger believers not to despise the weaker members because of their legalistic approach to the Christian life. Then he cautioned the weaker saints not to pass judgment on the stronger members because they were enjoying their freedom in Christ. But then he spoke to both groups and warned them not to do anything that would cause somebody else to stumble. When a "living stone" stops helping others, he starts to hinder others by his bad example.

So, the question we ask about "questionable things" is not "Can I do it safely?" but "If I do it, will it hurt somebody else?" The mature Christian can afford to set aside some of his rights so that he might show love to others and help them grow in the Lord. When our four children were small, my wife and I tried to be very careful about where we put knives and scissors, and about whether we closed and locked the doors. We were also careful about the kinds of books and magazines that were left around for little eyes to see.

Keep in mind that the mature Christian lovingly "gives in" to the weaker Christian *so that the weaker Christian will be kept safe and be allowed to mature. We must not allow the immature brother or sister to stay immature.* The whole purpose of Paul's admonitions in Romans 14–15 is to help the weak saint become a strong saint. Too often the weaker saints enjoy staying that way, like little children who will not grow up and accept new responsibilities.

Believers edify one another *by their speech* (Eph. 4:29). When God created the first man and woman, he gave them the wonderful gift of speech, a gift that we too often take for granted. Paul warned against "corrupt communication," which Greek scholar Kenneth Wuest translated "every word that is rotten and unfit for use" (*The New Testament: An Expanded Translation*, Eerdmans, 1961). Things that are rotten infect other things, and the decay starts to spread. One morsel of gossip, one off-color joke, one unloving statement, and Satan goes to work.

The best way to keep our speech from rotting is to make sure it is "seasoned with salt" (Col. 4:6). We must never say, "Now take this with a grain of salt!" *We* must put the "salt" into our speech by obeying God's Word, speaking the truth in love (Eph. 4:15), and sincerely seeking to edify others. Notice also that in both Ephesians 4:29 and Colossians 4:6 there is an emphasis on grace. We should follow the example of our Savior and have God's grace poured into our lips (Ps. 45:2).

As a radio Bible teacher, I receive a great deal of mail, and I must admit that some of it needs to be salted. On the other hand, I receive letters that edify my heart far more than my radio message edified the listener who wrote to me. Sometimes I hear from dedicated pastors or missionaries telling how God is answering prayer and building the church. Or it may be a note from a young couple sharing how God is blessing in the raising of their children. These letters minister grace to my heart because they magnify Jesus Christ.

We certainly can edify others *by our praying* (Col. 4:12). I like the New International Version translation of this verse: "Always wrestling in prayer for you, that you may stand firm in all the will of God, mature and fully assured." Prayer can be hard work. Sometimes it feels like you are in a wrestling match. As we pray for others, the Spirit of God can work in their lives and build them up in the faith. They will know the will of God and stand firmly in it. They will mature and have full assurance in their relationship to the Lord.

One of the greatest "tools" for edifying others is *the Word of God* (Acts 20:32). The Word of God is *able* to make us "wise unto salvation" (2 Tim. 3:15; James 1:21), and then, after we are saved, able to build us up and make us spiritually wealthy. There is an inheritance waiting for all believers who will take the Bible seriously and make it a vital part of their lives.

Vance Havner once said, "In a day when the living faith of the dead has become the dead faith of the living, just as America needs to get back to the Constitution, so the church needs to return to the cross and the Bible."

Finally, we edify one another *by exercising our spiritual gifts* (1 Cor. 14:12, 26). Some of the Corinthians thought that spiritual gifts were toys to play with, so they were using them in a most unspiritual manner and bringing division and disgrace to the church. Each believer has at least one spiritual gift; and as good stewards, we must use our gifts in the power of the Lord and for the glory of the Lord (1 Pet. 4:10-11). "Let all things be done unto edifying" (1 Cor. 14:26).

If each member of a local church would discover, dedicate, and discipline his or her spiritual gifts, and put them to work for the glory of God, we would see our churches grow and experience a new dynamic. It is my guess that about 15 percent of the members of the average church are really actively serving the Lord. The rest are spectators, cheerleaders, or critics. Sometimes the fault lies with the leadership of the church. It is so set in its ways that there is no opportunity for others to participate. The same people "hold" (but don't use) the same offices, and the new people (if there are any in the church) are not allowed to serve.

The church of Jesus Christ in this world is a glorious temple that God is building, though we cannot see the total edifice now. As "living stones," our responsibility is to find the place where God wants us to work and to be faithful in that place. We also have the privilege of praying for and encouraging other "living stones" in many parts of the world as we build together.

Anybody can go through life and work with Satan in tearing things down. Christians are working with Jesus Christ to help build his church, and what they build will last forever.

CHAPTER 7

A Dedicated Debtor

Thomas Jefferson warned his country that public debt was "the greatest of the dangers to be feared." He opposed the principle of "spending money to be paid by posterity" and called the practice "swindling futurity on a large scale." We wonder what Jefferson would say if he were alive today and knew that each American citizen was in debt about ten thousand dollars because the government could not balance its budget. And if he added to that amount the billions involved in personal consumer credit debts, Mr. Jefferson would no doubt conclude that both the future and the present had indeed been "swindled" on a large scale.

Of course, anybody in debt can always resort to the old adage, "Running into debt isn't so bad—it's running into your creditors that really causes trouble." However, after the laughter dies down, we have to confess that unpaid debts have a way of enslaving people and then demanding from them the last pound of flesh.

However, *spiritual* debts—the debts that we Christians owe because we belong to the family of God—rather than being a *burden*, are a *blessing*. The longer we are faithful to pay them, the more dividends we receive from the Lord.

A paradox? Of course! But a *practical* paradox that can lead to some wonderful joys in your Christian life.

Before we consider the six spiritual debts each Christian is obligated to pay, we must remind ourselves that *salvation is not a debt*. Salvation is a free gift from God and can be received only as a free gift (John 10:28-29 and 17:3; Rom. 5:15-18 and 6:23). People who try to earn their salvation by good works—even religious works—do not really understand the gospel of the grace of God. It was this misunderstanding that caused the nation of Israel to refuse the gift of salvation that Christ offered them (Rom. 9:30–10:13). Salvation is not by works but by grace, and to confuse the two is to rob God of glory and man of salvation (Rom. 11:6; Eph. 2:8-9).

1. Our Debt to a Lost World (Rom. 1:13-17)

A Jewish man asked his rabbi, "Why is it, whenever I ask you a question, you always answer with a question?" The rabbi replied, "So why shouldn't I?"

Cain tried that approach with God. "Am I my brother's keeper?" was his evasive reply to God's question, "Where is Abel thy brother?" (Gen. 4:9). This same reply is used by dishonest people today when they want to avoid the responsibility of helping others. Of course, the answer to Cain's question is, "Yes! You *are* your brother's keeper, so long as it is in your power to help your brother." To see others in need and do nothing to help them is to sin (James 2:14-17; 1 John 3:14-18).

In the first three chapters of the Roman epistle, Paul argued persuasively that everybody is a lost sinner and stands condemned before a holy God. This wholesale judgment includes the pagan Gentile (1:18-32) as well as the religious Jew (2:1–3:8). In fact, *the whole world* is guilty before God (3:9-20). Behind the veneer of modern so-called "civilization" beats a sinful heart that is in deliberate rebellion against God.

The good news is that God has provided salvation for a sinful world, and this glorious message ought to be motivation enough to encourage the church to get the Word out. The constraint of Christ's love (2 Cor. 5:14) and the conviction that the gospel really works (Rom. 1:16) motivated Paul to take the message of grace throughout the Roman Empire. An unbelieving humorist once said that missionaries were "sincere persons suffering from the meddler's itch," but that description is neither honest nor humorous. Evangelizing and meddling are not the same thing, for the missionary is under orders to carry the gospel to the whole world (Matt. 28:19-20; Mark 16:15).

We cannot pay this "spiritual debt" simply by giving money for missions and praying for missionaries, even though both of these ministries are important and essential. We must present *ourselves* to the Lord as living sacrifices (Rom. 12:1-2), available to him for whatever work he wants us to do, *starting at home*. The first missionaries began their witness right at home in Jerusalem and then enlarged their circle of ministry to include "the uttermost part of the earth" (Acts 1:8). Dr. Oswald J. Smith often said, "The light that shines the farthest will shine the brightest at home."

"Are people in today's world lost?" is not an academic question for theologians to debate in some ivory tower. The question is at the heart of the church's ministry, and the answer to the question is, "Yes, all men without Christ are lost." *And what are you doing about it*? Are you paying your debt by sharing the gospel with others?

2. Our Debt to the Holy Spirit of God (Rom. 8:12)

The Christian owes nothing to "the flesh," that is, the old nature that causes sin in our lives (Gal. 5:19-21; Mark 7:20-23). What good thing has the flesh ever done for us? Whatever the Bible has to say about the flesh is usually negative, and we had better accept this verdict. "For I know that in me (that is, in my flesh) dwelleth no good thing" (Rom. 7:18). "It is the spirit that quickeneth [gives life]; the flesh profiteth nothing" (John 6:63). "For we . . . have no confidence in the flesh" (Phil. 3:3).

Our debt is to the Holy Spirit who lives in us and makes our bodies his temple (1 Cor. 6:19-20). Just think of what the Holy Spirit has done for every child of God! He brought the Son of God into the world through the virgin womb of Mary (Luke 1:34-35; Isa. 7:14), empowered him in his life and ministry (Luke 4:1, 18), and strengthened him when he died for sinners on the cross (Heb. 9:14). The Spirit inspired the Word of God (2 Pet. 1:21; 2 Tim. 3:16) and then used that Word to convict us of sin and reveal the Savior (John 16:7-11). When we believed on Jesus Christ, the Holy Spirit entered our very being and gave us the assurance that we are the children of God (Rom. 8:14-16). He teaches us the Word of God and enables us to obey it (John 14:26). He gives us guidance as we pray (Rom. 8:26-27), and he empowers us to witness for Christ (Acts 1:8).

What an obligation we have to the Holy Spirit of God! But how do we go about paying this great debt? By devoting ourselves to the things that are important to the Holy Spirit.

For one thing, we must seek to glorify Christ, because that is the main ministry of the Holy Spirit. Jesus said, "He [the Spirit] shall glorify me" (John 16:14). The Spirit does not glorify himself; he always points to the Son of God. Any true work of the Spirit will always bring glory to Jesus Christ.

Since the Spirit lives in us, we pay our spiritual debt to him by taking good care of our bodies, which are his temples. This means a life separated from sin and yielded to God (2 Cor. 6:14–7:1).

The Spirit wrote the Word, and the central theme of that Word is Jesus Christ. Therefore, when we spend time reading the Bible and meditating on its truths, we are pleasing the Spirit and paying our debt to him. At the same time, we are giving the Spirit opportunity to transform us and make us more like the Lord Jesus Christ (2 Cor. 3:18).

Empowering believers to witness to the lost is another important ministry of the Spirit (Luke 24:45-49; Acts 1:8). As we yield to him and experience his fullness, we discover the power we need to share the gospel. But if we refuse to speak out for Christ, we grieve the Spirit and fail to pay our spiritual debt.

We can never fully repay the Holy Spirit for all the blessings he has brought to our lives and to the church, but we can at least acknowledge our indebtedness and start pleasing him.

3. Our Debt to Human Government (Rom. 13:1-6)

The fact that we have our citizenship in heaven ought to make us better citizens on earth, no matter under what form of government we may live. After all, when Paul wrote Romans 13, Nero was the emperor of Rome. "Render therefore to all their dues" (v. 7) implies that we have a debt to the government. The famous British historian Lord Acton said, "Christianity introduced no new forms of government, but a new spirit, which totally transformed the old ones." Martin Luther called government "a sign of divine grace."

When Paul says that "the powers that be are ordained of God," he is not suggesting that God is responsible for the election or the appointment of every government official. Certainly God is sovereign and can do what he pleases with a nation (Dan. 4:17; John 19:11; Acts 17:25-28). The phrase means that *governmental authority* has been established by God, so that the government official is actually "the minister of God" (Rom. 13:4, 6). As such, he deserves respect and obedience. We may not respect the person, but we must respect the office. (See 1 Pet. 2:11-17 for a parallel passage.)

The purpose of government is to protect and reward the

good and punish the evil. Governments that fail to respect human rights and protect human freedom are definitely contrary to the will of God. The Christian citizen must be true to his conscience, even if it means disobeying the law (Acts 4:18-20 and 5:29). It is possible to show respect to the authorities while at the same time refusing to obey a bad law. However, we must be sure that we are being true to God's Word and not just "riding a hobby" when we oppose the law.

Christians have a debt to government because this authority was given by God, and because the officials bear the sword and can punish those who break the law (Rom. 13:1-4). We should obey for conscience' sake (13:5-7) because we will one day answer to a higher authority. This means that Christians ought to pay their taxes and file honest tax returns. It also means that they should willingly, as a testimony for the Lord, obey all laws and regulations that do not violate their Christian conscience. "Live as free men, but do not use your freedom as a cover-up for evil; live as servants of God. Show proper respect to everyone: Love the brotherhood of believers, fear God, honor the king" (1 Pet. 2:16-17, NIV).

4. Our Debt to Our Neighbors (Rom. 13:8-10)

"Owe no man any thing, but to love one another" does not forbid the lending of money as a part of normal business, nor does it prohibit the honest use of credit. Jesus made this clear in two of his parables (Matt. 25:14-30; Luke 19:11-27). Paul was saying, "Your greatest debt is love—don't fall short of paying this debt!" If we would be as faithful to pay our "love debt" as we are in paying our other debts, the world would be a better place, the church would have a stronger testimony, and God would receive more glory.

The law is necessary, and government is essential to enforce the law; but Christians ought not to obey the law simply because they fear punishment. We should obey the law because we love others. In that sense, love is the fulfillment of the law. When you love people, you have no desire to lie about them, steal from them, or kill them. Your only desire is to do them good.

The first commandment is that you love God; the second is that you love your neighbor as yourself (Mark 12:28-31); and the third is that you keep the two together. "If a man say, I love God, and hateth his brother, he is a liar" (1 John 4:20). We can always try to evade the issue the way the lawyer did who asked Jesus, "And who is my neighbor?" (Luke 10:25-37). That is an old "debate tactic" by which you challenge your opponent to define his terms, while you try to think of a way out of the situation. In the parable of the Good Samaritan, Jesus cornered the lawyer by pointing out that the basic question is not Who is my neighbor? but To whom can I be a neighbor? There is a difference.

Some people live by lust and do anything that their hearts desire, even if what they do hurts others. Others live by the law and do exactly what it demands. But the Christian lives by love and seeks to glorify God by helping others. There may be situations in life that even the best statutes cannot cover, but love is always up-to-date and has the right answer. To be sure, practicing love costs something, and making the right decisions isn't always easy. There are times when it may seem safer to avoid our neighbor or pretend that we don't see the need; but those are the times when love grows the best. Not all of the solutions to life's problems are neat and tidy, but love can always make them easier and happier.

Where does this kind of sacrificial love come from? "God has poured out his love into our hearts by the Holy Spirit, whom he has given us" (Rom. 5:5, NIV). "But the fruit of the Spirit is love" (Gal. 5:17). Christian love is not a feeling that we turn on and off like a radio, only to discover that the power is low. Christian love simply means that we treat others the way God treats us, and we do this in the energy of the Holy Spirit. In one sense, it is the Lord Jesus Christ *in us* loving others *through us*, as we yield to him.

Christian love is practical; it doesn't just say words, it does what needs to be done. Christian love is personal; we don't minister by proxy. To be sure, we can't be everywhere, so we help to support others who work in needy corners of the world. But we don't fool ourselves into thinking that our donations for ministry elsewhere are substitutes for demonstrations of love right where we are. "The love of our neighbor is the only door out of the dungeon of self," wrote George MacDonald. It is a debt we must constantly pay—and thank God for the privilege.

5. Our Debt to Weaker Christians (Rom. 14:1–15:13)

"We then that are strong ought to bear the infirmities of the weak" (15:1). This is a evidently a solemn obligation, but who are the "strong" and the "weak," and how do the "strong" go about paying their debt to the "weak"?

The Christian assemblies in Rome were divided over observing special days and following special diets. It is likely that this division had national and racial origins because the Jewish believers hesitated to change their religious practices. Unlike the Gentiles, the Jewish Christians were accustomed to honor the Sabbath Day, obey the dietary laws, and celebrate the annual feasts (Lev. 23). It was a difficult thing for the Jews suddenly to step out of the yoke of the law (Acts 15:10) and into the freedom of God's grace. This is what helped to create the problem in the churches.

The "strong" Christians in Rome were those who believed God's Word and accepted their wonderful position in Jesus Christ. They rejoiced that they were not under the law, that Jesus Christ had fully met the demands of the law, and that their standing before God was wholly by grace. These people were strong in faith and in their conscience because they believed God's Word and acted upon it.

The "weak" Christians were saved people who had a difficult time accepting their freedom in Christ. They were still bound in mind and conscience to the traditions of their former religion. As yet, their conscience was not strong enough to make that step out of the security of law and into the liberty of grace.

Unfortunately, some of the "strong" saints despised their "weaker" brothers and sisters for not growing up. They disputed with them, hoping to argue them into a more mature Christian life. The "weak" believers condemned the "strong" ones for breaking God's law and setting a bad example, and the "strong" believers laughed at the "weak" ones for following religious diets and celebrating holy days. It was a bad situation all around and both groups were at fault.

We have a similar situation in the church today, except that the issues are different: fashions (hair and clothes), amusements, Sunday activities, separation from the world, and, in some places, even music and translations of the Bible. The strong Christians defend their liberty, only to be told by the weaker Christians that this so-called liberty is really nothing but anarchy and apostasy.

How do you solve this problem? Certainly not by issuing a new law and insisting that everybody obey it! No matter which side you champion, you would only alienate the other side and make the division worse.

Paul solved the problem by emphasizing the lordship of Jesus Christ and the believers' relationship to him. If Jesus is indeed the Lord of our lives, then we as individual believers ought to be able to live together in harmony, in spite of our differences.

Paul shared three simple steps for all of them to follow: (1) receive each other because Christ has received you, 14:1-12; (2) build each other up, don't tear each other down, 14:13-23; and (3) seek to please each other as you please Christ, 15:1-7. In 15:1 Paul made it clear that it is the strong Christian who has the greater obligation. The strong saint should seek to help the weaker brother to mature in the faith so that he then becomes strong and is able to strengthen others. Their differences must not be made a test of fellowship, church membership or spirituality. Rather, their personal differences must be looked upon as opportunities for *both sides* to practice patient love to the glory of God.

How many useless church fights would be avoided, and church splits prevented, if only God's people would stop majoring on the minor! We have a debt to pay to one another, to receive one another and to bear one another's infirmities in love, including any minor differences we may have concerning the Christian life. St. Augustine said it perfectly: "In essentials, unity; in nonessentials, liberty; in all things, charity."

6. Our Debt to the Jewish People (Rom. 15:25-29)

During his third missionary journey, Paul invested a good deal of time and energy visiting the Gentile churches he had founded and encouraging them to share in a special offering for the poor Jewish saints in Jerusalem. This offering was much more than a means of bringing relief to needy people, although that was paramount. It was also evidence of the oneness of God's church—Jews and Gentiles—and a beautiful opportunity for the Gentiles to show their love and appreciation to their Jewish brothers and sisters. (See Acts 24:17; 2 Cor. 8–9.)

Paul's logic was clear. The Jews gave the Gentiles spiritual blessings, so the Gentiles are debtors to the Jews and can best pay their debt by sharing material blessings. Paul used this same idea in Galatians 6:6-10 where he discussed giving within the local church.

Certainly the Gentiles *are* indebted to the Jews! The people of Israel gave to the idolatrous world the knowledge of the true God. They gave to the superstitious world the Bible, the Word of God; and to the sinful world, the nation of Israel gave the greatest gift of all, Jesus Christ the Savior. The first Christians were Jews, and the first missionaries were Jews. Were it not for the ministry of Paul, a Jew, the message of salvation would not have been carried to the Gentiles in the Roman Empire, and from there across the world.

President Ulysses Grant called the Jews "an intolerable nuisance," but President John Quincy Adams spoke the truth when he said, "The Hebrews have done more to civilize men than any other nation." What a debt we owe them!

How do we pay this debt? Perhaps the first step is to get rid of our prejudices and accept the Jews—saved and unsaved—as God's special treasure (Exod. 19:5). There can be no room for anti-Semitism in the heart of a Christian. Mark Twain called anti-Semitism "the swollen envy of pygmy minds," an excellent definition. Our Savior was a Jew, and our Bible is a Jewish book. So it is inconsistent for Christians to claim to love Christ and the Bible while at the same time showing prejudice against the Jews.

This does not mean that we must agree with everything that the nation of Israel does or says. Nor should we be so concerned about "to the Jew first" (Rom. 1:16; 2:6-11; 10:9-13) that we get out of balance in our ministry. It does mean that we recognize the Jews as God's chosen people whom he has not forsaken (Rom. 11) and for whom he has a great future.

It also means that we pray for the Jewish people and seek to win them to Christ (Rom. 10). Those who bless Israel, God has promised to bless (Gen. 12:-3). "Pray for the peace of Jerusalem: they shall prosper that love thee" (Ps. 122:6).

Gentile Christians can pay their debt to Israel by sharing love and practical help with their Jewish neighbors. Many Jewish people live in fear and have the mistaken idea that

Christians are their enemies. Of course, some Jews equate "Christian" with "Gentile," and this unfortunate mistake results in unnecessary ill will. There are many ways that believers can minister to their Jewish friends and, at the same time, share the love of Christ. It is not necessary to preach to them all the time or drown them in Christian literature. We can win the right to be heard by showing practical love and by being "living epistles" of Christ that they can read.

Paul looked at this special "relief offering" as a debt to be paid (Rom. 15:27), and also as a sacrifice offering to the Lord. The Greek word translated "minister" in Romans 15:27 means "a priestly ministry." It gives us our English word *liturgy*. The offering from the Gentile churches was a "spiritual sacrifice" on the altar, offered to the Lord (Phil. 4:18).

The offering was also "fruit" (15:28), not "loot." The Gentile Christians were not forced to give. They shared what they had because of the life of Christ within them. The Spirit-filled Christian enjoys giving and does not have to be bribed or bullied. Giving is a "fruit" that is produced by the life-giving Spirit within.

Financial debts can ruin us, but paying our spiritual debts should make us better Christians and more useful citizens. It was this deep sense of spiritual obligation that motivated Paul in his life and ministry, and it should also motivate us.

"I am debtor," he wrote. "I am ready to preach the gospel. I am not ashamed of the gospel."

Will you become one of God's dedicated debtors?

CHAPTER 8

A Soldier in God's Army

Dwight L. Moody did not want his song leader Ira Sankey to use "Onward Christian Soldiers" in their evangelistic meetings. It was all right for Sankey to have the crowd sing "Hold the Fort, for I Am Coming" but not "Onward Christian Soldiers." Why? Well, Mr. Moody thought that the church as he knew it did not look or act like an army of Christian soldiers, and maybe he was right.

However, the Apostle Paul often used military imagery in his letters; and, thanks to the ever-present Roman legions, those images were very meaningful to the recipients of his epistles. No doubt today there are believers in totalitarian nations who understand some of these references better than do the believers living in free countries.

Mr. Moody had a Quaker background, and Quakers are traditionally nonmilitant. But even Moody would have to admit that there is definitely a military side to what the Bible teaches about God and the Christian life. "The Lord is a man of war!" sang Moses and his people after they had crossed the Red Sea (Exod. 15:3). "The Lord strong and mighty," sang David, "the Lord mighty in battle"(Ps. 24:8).

Even our Savior is pictured as a conqueror riding a white horse (Ps. 45:3-7; Rev. 19:11-21).

Of course, we must remember that the Christian's warfare is in the realm of the spiritual (Eph. 6:10-12), and we should use only spiritual armor and spiritual weapons in our battles (Eph. 6:13-18; 2 Cor. 10:3-5). Peter tried to use a sword to defend the Lord, and Jesus severely rebuked him (John 18:10-11). At Pentecost, Peter used the "sword of the Spirit" and turned three thousand enemies into brothers. That's the way to do battle.

Using Paul's admonitions to Timothy as the basis for our study, let us examine a number of topics and see what it means today to be a "Christian soldier."

1. The Soldier's Enlistment

Whether we like it or not, we were "drafted" when we trusted Jesus Christ as our Savior and were born again into the family of God. Every child of God is a soldier in God's army, either a good one or a bad one. In fact, the very first mention of the church in the New Testament (Matt. 16:18) includes the military image. of conflict: "And the gates of hell shall not prevail against it." It is the picture of an army storming the gates and conquering the city.

The city gate was the place of official business and civic authority (see Ruth 4:1ff.; Deut. 21:19ff.); so Jesus was saying to Peter, "My church will overcome all the authority in the realm of death." (The Greek word translated "hell" in the King James Version is *hades*, the realm of the dead; see Job 38:17 and Isa. 38:10.) As members of the army of the Lord, we follow a Commander who has "all authority" (Matt. 28:18), including authority over Satan, sin, death, and hell.

No sooner were the people of Israel delivered from Egypt when they found themselves fighting a battle (Exod. 17:8-16). Whether they liked it or not, they were soldiers! But God gave them victory through the prayers of Moses

on the mountain and the leadership of Joshua on the battlefield. The people learned a new name for God—"Jeho-
vah-Nissi," which means, "The Lord is our banner." Just
as Moses on the mountain interceded for Israel, so Jesus
Christ in heaven today intercedes for his church. But, unlike Moses, he never gets weary and his intercession never
ends (Heb. 7:23-28).

As Christian soldiers, we are following a Commander
who has been rejected by the world. As far as the unsaved
world is concerned, Jesus Christ is a loser and not worth
following. Christians are very much like the men who followed David during his years of exile and rejection: "And
every one that was in distress, and every one that was in
debt, and every one that was discontented, gathered themselves unto him; and he became a captain over them"
(1 Sam. 22:2). Our Commander has given us joy for distress, forgiveness for indebtedness, and deep satisfaction
for our discontent; and we find being associated with him
an exciting and enriching experience.

When it comes to following Jesus Christ, it is impossible
to be neutral. "He that is not with me is against me; and
he that gathereth not with me scattereth abroad" (Matt.
12:30). Moses' cry still goes out: "Who is on the Lord's
side?" (Exod. 32:26).

2. The Soldier's Enablement

We have no strength of our own, so we must "be strong in
the grace that is in Christ Jesus" (2 Tim. 2:1). This does
not mean that we neglect basic training and maneuvers,
because every believer wants to be at his best for his Lord.
The expression, "Exercise thyself rather unto godliness"
(1 Tim. 4:7) suggests that the soldier has to do his part if
he is to keep in shape. The point is that we don't depend
on our own strength, experience, or expertise. We depend
on God's grace.

"Without me ye can do nothing" (John 15:5). This statement explains why our Commander-in-Chief puts us through difficult "maneuvers." He wants us to discover for ourselves just how weak we really are. He already knows, but the trouble is, we don't. The first step toward spiritual victory is simply accepting as true *for ourselves* what God says about us in his Word. Once we have done that, we can start depending on the grace of God. Keep in mind that God's grace doesn't work *in spite of* us, or even *instead of* us; his grace works *in* us and *through* us. We have to cooperate by yielding to God and trusting him.

Our God is "the God of all grace" (1 Pet. 5:10), and his throne is a throne of grace (Heb. 4:16). Because we belong to him, we can come to his throne of grace and get the help we need when we need it. Oswald Chambers called grace "the overflowing favor of God," and that is just what it is. "He giveth more grace" (James 4:6)—and he does! God has all the grace there is and all the grace you need.

Our enemy, Satan, doesn't want us to depend on God's grace because it means defeat for him every time. Satan wants us to depend on ourselves and to fight with the weapons of the world. Our strong weapons are the Word of God and prayer (Acts 6:4; Eph. 6:17-18). When Satan attacked Jesus in the wilderness, the Savior overcame him with the Word of God (Matt. 4:1-11). Satan, the liar and deceiver, cannot stand long before God's truth.

Moses tried to fight the Lord's battles without using the Lord's weapons, and he failed miserably (Exod. 2:11-14). There was nothing wrong with Moses's head (Acts 7:22) or heart, but there was something seriously wrong with his hand. God had to put him on the backside of the desert with sheep for forty years, just to teach him how to depend on the grace of God.

The believer needs God's grace in order to be able to "endure hardness as a good soldier of Jesus Christ" (2 Tim. 2:3). He must be able, without shame, to be a "partaker of the afflictions of the gospel according to the power of God" (2 Tim. 1:8). The person who permanently goes AWOL is proving that he was never really enlisted at all; for all of God's soldiers, in spite of their failures, are eventually overcomers (1 John 5:1-5).

When I pastored the Moody Church in Chicago, I often heard the old-timers talking about the ministry of Paul Rader, who pastored the church from 1915 to 1921 and saw thousands come to Christ. I began to read about Mr. Rader and to collect what books he had written that were still available. He was indeed a powerful preacher with a way of expressing Bible truth that really reached the common man.

This is what he said about God's grace: "Manifold grace means that it is not just one blessing, but there are thousands to come, one after another. The joy you have multiplies the joys to come; the victory you have in Christ multiplies the coming conquests." If that truth doesn't help us on the battlefield, then we need to rediscover the power of the grace of God!

"Finally, my brethren, be strong in the Lord, and in the power of his might" (Eph. 6:10).

3. The Soldier's Enlightenment

The training manual for the Christian soldier is the Word of God. "And the things that thou hast heard of me among many witnesses, the same commit thou to faithful men, who shall be able to teach others also" (2 Tim. 2:2).

During the Cuban missile crisis of October 1962, President Kennedy and his staff were doing their utmost to prevent a war with Russia. In the dramatization, "The Missiles of October," Secretary of Defense Robert McNamara asks a naval officer if anybody on the U.S. ships could speak Russian, just in case one of their ships had to be boarded. The officer is very upset that anyone would question the navy's ability to handle a problem at sea. He reminds McNamara that the navy has a manual to guide them and tell them exactly what to do in every emergency.

McNamara's reply is, "I don't care what John Paul Jones would do! I want to know what *you* plan to do!"

Military training manuals may become outdated, but not the Word of God. "For ever, O Lord, thy word is settled in heaven" (Ps. 119:89). We need new translations of the Word of God because language changes, but we do not need a new Word of God. God has spoken and that settles it (Heb. 1:1-2).

The better you know your Bible, the better you will know the enemy and what his strategy is as he seeks to defeat you. From Genesis 3 to Revelation 20, Satan's character and subtle devices are clearly explained, so that no Christian soldier need be confused. The enemy has done nothing new since he tempted Eve; all he does is present the same old thing in a new disguise.

The better you know your Bible, the better you will know yourself and what God wants to do for you. Also, the better you will know your Savior and what he can do to help make you a conqueror. Your Bible is God's gift to you (John 17:14) and, next to the gift of eternal life, it is the greatest gift you possess.

"O how love I thy law! it is my meditation all the day. Thou through thy commandments hast made me wiser than mine enemies: for they are ever with me" (Ps. 119:97-98).

4. The Soldier's Entanglement

"No one serving as a soldier gets involved in civilian affairs—he wants to please his commanding officer" (2 Tim. 2:4, NIV). I read about a Civil War soldier who had been a watchmaker in civilian life and set himself up in business in his camp, repairing watches and earning extra money. One day the bugle blew and his company was ordered to be ready to move within the hour.

"I can't do it!" the watchmaker lamented. "I have too much work to do and I'll lose my customers!"

Before we criticize him, let's examine our own lives and find out what kind of situation we would be in if the trumpet were to blow and God's soldiers were called up.

Jesus insisted on total commitment and warned, "No man can serve two masters" (Matt. 6:24). "A double minded man is unstable in all his ways" (James 1:8). The men and women in the Bible who conquered were those who gave themselves unreservedly to the Lord and, in spite of their mistakes and failings, devotedly tried to please him. "We are not trying to please men but God, who tests our hearts" (1 Thess. 2:4, NIV).

What did Paul mean by "civilian affairs" ("the affairs of this life")? He was probably referring to those good but not important things that distract the soldier from his number one task of obeying and pleasing his commander. In the eyes of civilians, these things might not appear to be wrong. But in the eyes of the commander, these "good things" take the soldier away from the better things and the best things.

It was double-mindedness that led to Israel's defeat at Ai after their great victory at Jericho (Josh. 7). Joshua instructed the army to dedicate to God all the spoil from Jericho, but Achan disobeyed. He saw a "goodly Babylonish garment, and two hundred shekels of silver, and a wedge of gold of fifty shekels weight" (Josh. 7:21), and he took them and hid them in his tent. As a result, Israel failed in their first attempt to conquer Ai, and thirty-six of their men were killed.

The Greek word translated "entangle" also means "to entwine or braid the hair." This reminds us of Samson, that mighty soldier, who finally lost his power because he got entangled with a sinful woman who braided his hair and gradually led him into shame and defeat (Judg. 16:4ff.). A similar thing happened to Lot, Abraham's nephew: he looked toward Sodom (Gen. 13:10), then pitched his tent toward Sodom (Gen. 13:12), and finally moved into Sodom (14:12). Little by little, he got entangled and stopped pleasing the Lord; and the results were disastrous (Gen. 19:15-38).

How do we keep from getting entangled? By seeking to please Jesus Christ in our every motive, word and action. We are supposed to "walk and to please God" (1 Thess. 4:1). When a soldier makes a decision, the big question is not "Is it safe?" or "Is it popular?" but "Is it right? Is this what my commander wants me to do?" If we, by faith, obey our Commander, then the consequences are in his capable hands and we don't have to worry.

Five times in 1 Timothy, Paul used the Greek word *parangello*, which means "to hand down a military order which must be obeyed." In 1:3 he told Timothy to "charge [order] some that they teach no other doctrine." In 4:11, he admonished young Timothy, "These things command [order] and teach." As the spiritual leader in the church, he was expected to give his people God's "marching orders." "And these things give in charge" (5:7). Pass God's orders down through the troops. "I give thee charge," he reminded Timothy (6:13), and then told him to "Charge them that are rich in this world" (6:17).

In other words, the church should receive God's orders from his Word just the way an army receives orders from their commander: with respect, alertness, and the intention to obey. If the men and women in the armed forces treated their orders with the same carelessness the average Christian treats God's Word—they would probably all be court martialed!

5. The Soldier's Encouragement

The Christian life is not easy. There are many battles and our enemy is extremely powerful and subtle. Sometimes the dedicated Christian soldier feels like he or she is standing alone. What kind of encouragement do we have from the Lord? The greatest encouragement is that Jesus Christ has already won the fight and we need only follow him by faith. We are not fighting *for* victory but *from* victory. "But thanks be to God, who always leads us in triumphal procession in Christ and through us spreads everywhere the fragrance of the knowledge of him" (2 Cor. 2:14, NIV).

The picture here is that of the "Roman triumph," which was Rome's version of our modern ticker-tape parade. Whenever one of their commanders returned home from battle, he was welcomed publicly with a "triumph," *if* he qualified. To begin with, he must have won a complete victory on foreign soil, with at least five thousand enemy soldiers slain. Also, his victory had to result in new territory gained for the Roman Empire and considerable treasure brought home.

The parade followed a traditional route, with the hero riding in a special chariot, his soldiers and officers near him to share in the glory. Also, the spoils of battle would be on display, carried by slaves or by soldiers in chariots. The priests would be there with their censers spreading the fragrance of incense. But even more, the enemy captives would be in the parade and eventually end up in the coliseum where they would entertain the celebrants by fighting with the lions. What a victory celebration!

Paul tells us that Jesus Christ has won a complete victory on foreign soil (our world) and returned to heaven in a triumphal procession (Eph. 4:8; Col. 2:15). He has won the victory, claimed the spoils, and is sharing both with us! As Christians, we smell the incense of life and victory. But the lost world smells the incense of defeat and death (2 Cor. 2:15-16). To the captives in the Roman parade, that incense meant death; but to the conquering soldiers, it meant life and glory.

There is no reason for us to feel or act defeated, for we are following in his train. "But thanks be to God, which giveth us the victory through our Lord Jesus Christ" (1 Cor. 15:57).

6. The Soldier's Equipment

The key text here is Ephesians 6:10-18 where "the whole armor of God" is described. The purpose of this armor is to enable the soldier to "stand" before the battle (v. 11), "withstand" during the battle (v. 13), and "stand" after the victory (v. 14). The first is defensive and the second is offensive, and both are important.

As we study the various parts of the Christian's spiritual armor, we should keep in mind that each part reveals two things: (1) an area of need in our lives, and (2) a strategy Satan uses in attacking that area. Paul wrote these words to Christians in a local church, not to members of a Satanist society. The devil and his angels work *within the church* as they seek to influence the lives of believers. Even the Apostle Peter was influenced by Satan and didn't realize it (Matt. 16:21-23; and note 2 Cor. 11:1-4).

The *girdle of truth* speaks of the believer's life "pulled together" by God's truth. Instead of duplicity, there is integrity. The Roman soldier's girdle was more than a belt; it was more like a leather apron that helped cover the lower part of the body and tie everything together. We must beware of being double-hearted (Matt. 6:19-21) and double-minded (James 1:8) and trying to serve two masters (Matt. 6:24). We must love God with all that we have and not hold anything back (Matt. 12:30).

The *breastplate of righteousness* symbolizes the righteousness of Jesus Christ that has been put to our account (imputed) because we have trusted him as our Savior (Rom. 3:19-24). Satan is the accuser of God's people (Rev. 12:10; Zech. 3); he enjoys reminding us of our past sins and making us feel guilty. Once we start listening to him we become defenseless. But if we remember that we have Christ's righteousness as our own, we can silence him. The soldier needs to be grounded in solid Bible doctrine and know what salvation really means.

The *shoes of peace* have to do with the Christian soldier's standing. Good sandals, usually with hobnails on the soles, were important to the Roman soldier, for they gave him a firm footing as he faced the enemy. What gives us our firm footing? The gospel of Jesus Christ. (See 1 Cor. 15:1-5; Rom. 5:1-2; Gal. 5:1.) Because we know where we stand, we are able to face the enemy and not run away. Because we have "peace with God," we are not afraid to declare war. Satan is certainly not a peacemaker. His aim is to create problems and tear things apart. The Christian soldier is the true "ambassador of peace," bringing the message of peace to a world that is at war with God.

The *shield of faith* protects the Christian soldier from the "fiery darts" of Satan, those wicked thoughts that he throws at us. He has thrown these darts at me even while I have been preaching the Word. We can't stop him from throwing them, but we can stop them and extinguish them by using faith in God's Word. The Roman soldier's shield was quite large, perhaps two feet by four feet, made of wood, and covered with heavy cloth or leather. When the believer today puts his faith in God—his person, his promises, and his power—then he is safe from these fiery darts.

The *helmet of salvation* protects the soldier's head just as the breastplate of righteousness protects his heart. Satan is a deceiver and we need to *think* like saved people and have the mind of Christ (2 Cor. 11:1-4). The helmet is also called "the hope of salvation" (1 Thess. 5:8), the promise of Christ's coming again. Satan would like us to forget that "blessed hope" because he knows that the promise of Christ's return is a motivation for purity and strength. "Hold the fort, for I am coming," we sing, in remembering this truth.

The *sword of the Spirit* is, of course, the Word of God (Heb. 4:12), and this is used in conjunction with *prayer* to defeat the evil one (see Acts 6:4). We are reminded again of Moses on the mountain praying and Joshua and his army on the battlefield wielding their swords (Exod. 17:8-16). Material swords are dead and grow dull, but our spiritual sword is living and gets sharper the more we use it. The soldier doesn't give power to the sword—the sword gives power to the soldier. A material sword cuts the outer person, but God's sword pierces the inner person and exposes everything just as it is. A material sword brings death to living people, but the sword of the Spirit brings life to people who are dead in their sins.

All of this is interesting, but how do we make it work in our daily experience? To begin with, each day we must, by faith, put on all the pieces of the armor; and we do this through prayer. The song says:

Put on the gospel armor,
Each piece put on with prayer.

Ephesians 6:18 says literally, "By means of the instrumentality of every prayer." In other words, it is through prayer, by faith, that we put on each piece and then put each piece to work whenever the enemy attacks us. The Holy Spirit gives us the discernment and the power to protect ourselves defensively and then attack Satan offensively, just as the Spirit helped Jesus to defeat Satan in the wilderness (Matt. 4:1-11).

The defensive pieces provided by God require no action on our part except to put them on by faith and trust God to make them work. However, the two offensive pieces—the Word of God and prayer—need our cooperation if they are going to be effective. We must read God's Word, study it, meditate on it, hide it in our hearts, and by faith claim it and use it when the enemy strikes. This is where "spiritual discipline" comes in, because God will not do all of this for us. We must take time to pray and then maintain an attitude of prayer all day long. Some Christians call their daily devotional time their "morning watch," which sounds like a soldier reporting for duty.

Being a soldier of Jesus Christ is a serious thing, for we are fighting the battles of the Lord. It is also an exciting thing, for we never know what will happen next. But one thing is sure: as long as we obey Jesus Christ, victory is certain.

Bernard of Clairvaux is remembered as a devoted mystical man who wrote, among other things, "Jesus, the Very Thought of Thee." But Bernard of Clairvaux knew what it was to battle the enemy, and this is what he wrote: "If Christ is with us, who is against us? You can fight with confidence where you are sure of victory. With Christ and for Christ, victory is certain."

CHAPTER 9

A Runner in the Race

When I was a teenager attending Youth for Christ rallies, one of our "Christian heroes" was Gil Dodds, "the flying parson." For eleven years, he held the record for the indoor mile. As track coach at Wheaton College in Illinois, he turned out one winning team after another. The Eric Liddell of my day, Gil Dodds could really run, and he did it to the glory of God.

I suppose I was more interested in him than in some of the other Christian athletes because about the only athletic thing I could do as a teenager was to run. Youth for Christ football heroes like Glenn Wagner and Bob Davenport, or pole vaulters like Bob Richards, didn't capture my attention. I was too light for football and didn't enjoy the game anyway. And as for pole vaulting, I might just as well try to fly. But running, well, that was something I could do.

Imagine my surprise as a young Christian when I discovered that the Apostle Paul in his letters often mentioned various sports, including running! Of course, both the Greeks and the Romans in Paul's day emphasized athletics, so Paul was simply taking advantage of their interests. If Paul were alive on earth today, he would probably read the sports page of the daily newspaper and use what he read somewhere in his sermons.

According to J. S. Howson in his book *The Metaphors of St. Paul*, "The gymnasium, or place of training, and the stadium, or ground for running, were among the most conspicuous and most frequented spots in the architecture and embellishment of the cities." Howson stated that sporting events "were almost a religion among the Greeks," which sounds very modern to us. So, wherever Paul ministered, he met people who knew about athletics and he took advantage of this knowledge as he ministered the Word of God.

The Romans considered sports a good source of entertainment, while the Greeks saw athletic events as a means of enrichment. "A healthy mind in a healthy body" was one of their goals. Each Greek boy was enrolled very early in the gymnasium and was expected to learn the basics of running, wrestling, boxing, and swimming, with perhaps some rowing, weight lifting, and occasional ball games thrown in for the sake of variety and challenge.

Some Famous Runners

The first "Christian runner" we meet in the New Testament is John the Baptist, and it was Paul himself who told us about him. In his sermon in the Antioch synagogue, Paul said of John the Baptist, "And as John fulfilled his course" (Acts 13:25). The verb means "to finish running the race." God gave John a special "track" on which to run, and he ran his race successfully and finished the work God gave him to do. To the unbelieving people, John may have appeared to be a failure. In fact, John may have considered himself a failure! But Jesus made it clear that John was a winner no matter what anybody said (Matt. 11:1-15).

Paul used the image of the race to describe his own ministry. His great desire was to finish his course with joy (Acts 20:24; note also Gal. 2:2; Phil. 2:16; 3:12-14). Paul did finish his course with joy and victory, to the glory of God (2 Tim. 4:7-8). The phrase "fought a good fight" does not refer either to war or boxing. It refers to the exertion of the runner as he nears the end of the race and sees the goal ahead. In other words, Paul is reminding us that faithful Christian ministry is not easy. It takes courage and strength to run the Christian race successfully.

"I wish I had continued at college," a friend told the great Samuel Johnson, compiler of the English dictionary. When Johnson asked his friend to explain, the man replied, "Because I think I should have had a much easier life than mine has been. I should have been a parson, and had a good living."

"No, sir," replied Johnson emphatically, "I do not envy a clergyman's life as an easy life, nor do I envy the clergyman who makes it an easy life."

Paul would have agreed with Samuel Johnson, for he often used the Greek verb *agonizomai* when referring to the Christian life. It means "to fight, to have conflict, to labor, to contend," and it describes the athlete giving his best as he competes in the games. You will find the word used to describe Paul's ministry in Philippians 1:30, Colossians 1:29 and 2:1, and 1 Thessalonians 2:2. He related it to prayer in Colossians 4:12 and Romans 15:30; for true prayer is a demanding thing.

Our Lord Jesus Christ is the certainly greatest "runner" of all. According to Hebrews 12:1-2, he laid aside everything to run the race to the glory of God (Phil. 2:1-11). He could reach his goal only by dying on a cross, so the race was not an easy one. Like a good runner with his eye on the goal, our Lord "steadfastly set his face to go to Jerusalem," and he would not be detoured (Luke 9:51; Isa. 50:7). What an example for us to follow!

The Winners
Very few athletes win by accident. Winning is the result of hard work, and that includes long hours of practicing and a life-style of serious discipline. Taking a few pages out of

Paul's "Christian athletes' notebook," we see some of the essentials for winning the Christian race.

To begin with, winning athletes *enjoy the game*. They may not enjoy all the difficult preparation that goes into the game, and they surely don't enjoy losing. But the thrill of the game is in their blood and nothing will keep them away. Paul gave expression to this attitude when he said, "But none of these things move me . . . so that I might finish my course with joy" (Acts 20:24). Jesus ran the race triumphantly "for the joy that was set before him" (Heb. 12:2). The joyful runner has already won *on the inside*.

"I think I feel emotions more than most players," said tennis star Chris Evert Lloyd. "I have a drive, a burning desire to win every time I step on a court." If you decide you are going to lose, you probably will.

It is worth noting that the word *amateur* comes from the Latin *amator* and means "a lover." The amateur athlete participates in a sport because he loves the sport, but many professional athletes feel the same way. They may receive big salaries and a lot of publicity, but it is the love of the game that helps to keep them going.

It takes more than love or getting "psyched up" to win the race; it also *demands discipline*. Paul cautioned Timothy, "Have nothing to do with godless myths and old wives' tales; rather, train yourself to be godly. For physical training is of some value, but godliness has value for all things, holding promise for both the present life and the life to come" (1 Tim. 4:7-8, NIV).

The Greek word translated "train" gives us our English word *gymnasium*. Paul was contrasting spiritual "exercise" with the exercise of the body. He didn't condemn physical exercise. He only pointed out that spiritual discipline pays dividends in this life and in the life to come. In other words, he was saying, "Timothy, there's nothing wrong with going to the gymnasium in Ephesus and working out every day. But please put as much discipline into your spiritual life as you do your physical life. It will produce more lasting good."

My wife and I belong to a health club, but I must confess that she is much more diligent about attending and using the facilities than I am. I tell our friends that she rides the bicycle and I sit in the side car and read a book. Frankly, it is intimidating for me to go to the club, especially when I meet the people who have made "physical culture" their number one occupation. They swim, run the track, lift weights, ride the bicycles, and then work their way through the special equipment that only the experts tackle. As I watch them, I ask myself, "Do I put as much discipline into building my Christian life as they do into developing their bodies?"

However, we must never think that the "body" and the "soul" can be separated when it comes to Christian living. What a believer does with his body is as much a part of the spiritual life as what he does in his devotional time or how he uses his talents or his money. The artificial division we make between "physical" and "spiritual" is not at all biblical. Presenting our bodies to the Lord is a part of our "spiritual worship" (Rom. 12:1-2), and what we do with our bodies will have a direct bearing on how God will reward us one day.

Paul wrote, "But I discipline my body and bring it into subjection, lest, when I have preached to others, I myself should become disqualified" (1 Cor. 9:27, NKJV). The apostle saw himself as a herald at the Olympic Games, calling the contestants to run the race with him. As a Christian, Paul was just another runner; but as a chosen apostle, he was like an official at the games. What was his fear? That in some way he might break the rules and find himself put out of the race. The Greek word *adokimos* does not mean "condemned," as though Paul were afraid of losing the gift of salvation. It means "disqualified, disapproved." This would mean humiliation, ejection from the game, and loss of reward.

Some believers today smile at the spiritual disciplines of the saints of past ages, and perhaps some of these disciplines were extreme. But there is no substitute for physical, mental, and spiritual discipline if you want to be a winning Christian. After all, Jesus calls us to a life of discipleship (Luke 14:25-35); and *discipleship* and *discipline* go together. "Discipline is the soul of an army," George Washington wrote to the Virginia regiments in 1759. "It makes small numbers formidable; procures success to the weak, and esteem to all."

Samson is an example of a believer who did not practice discipline (see Judg. 13–16). Instead of keeping his body under control, Samson lived to please himself, and the consequences were tragic. His sad career has been duplicated more than once by naive people who defend their sins and lack of self-control as "enjoying freedom in Christ." Such "freedom" is the worst kind of bondage.

Winning athletes *obey the rules of the game*. Paul reminded Timothy that "if anyone competes in athletics, he is not crowned unless he competes according to the rules" (2 Tim. 2:5, NKJV). The Greeks not only had rules for the games, but they also had rules for the contestants as they *trained* for the games. If a contestant showed up who had broken training, he was immediately disqualified.

In 1912 the American athlete Jim Thorpe won the decathlon and the pentathlon at the Olympic Games in Stockholm. But the next year he had to give back his gold medals because it was discovered he had played professional baseball in 1911. He had won the events but had broken the rules, so he lost his prizes. At the 1984 Olympic Games in Los Angeles the committee restored his awards. But even this did not alter that fact that Thorpe had broken the rules.

When Paul wrote to Timothy, "I have kept the faith" (2 Tim. 4:7), he meant, "I have obeyed the rules." As he ministered, Paul's concern was to be faithful, not just successful. For that matter, many people no doubt felt Paul was a failure, when in the eyes of God, Paul was a success.

We live at a time when many different religious leaders

are "doing their own thing," and some of them appear to be very popular and successful. But time will tell how many of them have faithfully obeyed the Word of God and kept the rules. Crowds, budgets, media exposure, and statistics will mean nothing in heaven if they do not hear, "Well done good and faithful servant"!

Winning athletes *stick to their calling and seek to do it well.* They would heartily approve of Paul's "this one thing I do" (Phil. 3:12-14) because concentration and consecration lead to victory. If during his period of training the athlete competes with himself, then he will be prepared to compete with the challengers.

"Forgetting those things which are behind" is an important part of running a winning race. *You can't successfully run forward if you are looking backward.* The contestant who takes his eyes off the goal is in danger of losing both his direction and his motivation. He must not be distracted by the crowd, either their cheers or jeers; and he must not let the other runners distract him. Nor should he look back inwardly and depend on past successes or be discouraged by the memory of past failures. Each race is unique and demands the very best.

God has a "lane" for each of his children to run in and a goal for each one to reach. We are not competing with each other. We are competing with ourselves and striving to do better as we run the race. Remember, we are not running the race in order to get into heaven. It is only through faith in Jesus Christ that our sins are forgiven and we have the assurance of heaven (John 14:1-6). In the Greek and Roman games, the contestants had to be citizens; no slaves or outsiders were permitted to compete. In the Christian race, each runner is a citizen of heaven (Phil. 3:20) and is running to bring glory to the Lord.

Early in my own ministry, I tried to run in too many lanes. I was a pastor, a youth speaker, a gospel magician, an evangelist, a writer, a Bible teacher, even a standup comedian at banquets. Then the Lord began to show me the importance of "this one thing I do." I discovered that I did not have the evangelistic gift and that youth work was not my best ministry. Gradually I dropped the gospel magic and comedy, and I began to concentrate on teaching the Word of God in public and through the printed page. That was when God really began to bless.

Years ago, when I was a teenager, Dr. Torrey M. Johnson, one of the founders of Youth for Christ, said to me, "Son, find that one thing you do that God blesses, *and stick with it!*" That was wise counsel, and I recommend it to you.

Winning athletes *think about the goal and the prize.* In one of the churches I pastored, one of our fine members was football coach at a local high school. He had played football at Ohio State and had even played in the Rose Bowl. So, to us, he was something of a local hero. Best of all, he had a good testimony for the Lord.

During one season, his team played poorly and was constantly at the bottom in the high school standings. Once I tried to cheer him up by quoting Grantland Rice, "He marks not that you won or lost but how you played the game."

"That's not the way I learned it," he replied grimly. "The way I learned it, winning isn't everything—it's the *only* thing."

I learned later that he was paraphrasing Vince Lombardi who said, "Winning isn't everything, but wanting to win is." Either way, we get the point: the dedicated athlete wants to win and will do his best to achieve victory. If he loses, he will learn from that loss and get ready to win the next time.

This explains why Paul wrote: "Do you not know that those who run in a race all run, but one receives the prize? Run in such a way that you may obtain it" (1 Cor. 9:24, NKJV). In the Olympic Games, only a few can be winners; but in the Christian race, *all of us can be winners!*

Many of us were thrilled to watch Mark Spitz become

the first athlete in history to win seven gold medals at an Olympic Game (Munich, 1972). We were not surprised to learn that Mark and his father had spent many years together training for that event. When Mark was just a boy, Arnold Spitz would repeatedly say to him, "How many lanes in the pool, Mark?"

Mark would reply, "Six."

Then Mr. Spitz would ask, "How many lanes *win,* Mark?"

The boy would reply, "One."

That is good training for an Olympics contestant, but not for a Christian runner in the race of faith, for in the Christian race *all six lanes could be winners.* In the Greek games, unlike our modern Olympics, only the first place winners were counted. If you came in second or third, you were ignored. But that is not the way God deals with his runners. *Every Christian can be a first place winner!* Why? Because we are not competing with each other; we are competing with ourselves. God will not judge me on the basis of what Charles Haddon Spurgeon did, but on the basis of what I did with the opportunities and gifts he gave to me. Spurgeon had his "lane" and his goal, and I have mine. This is, to me, one of the greatest encouragements in the Christian race, and it saves us from a lot of intimidation.

Paul went on to make another contrast between the Greek races and the race of faith: the Greek winners received only a fading wreath, while the Christian receives a crown of glory that will never fade. "Now they do it to obtain a perishable crown, but we for an imperishable crown" (1 Cor. 9:25, NKJV).

Of course, just being able to compete in the games is a reward in itself, for it means that the athlete has reached a high level of achievement. "The most important thing in the Olympic Games is not to win," states the official Olympic Creed, "but to take part. . . . The essential thing is not to have conquered but to have fought well." The motto of

the Olympics is "Faster—higher—braver!" Even apart
from medals and cheers is the strength and coordination of
the contestant's body.

So with the Christian: even if our Father never gave us
any rewards, just growing in grace and becoming more
like Jesus Christ is really a reward in itself. However, in his
grace, he will reward us, "and then shall every man have
praise of God" (1 Cor. 4:5).

Each winner in the Greek games not only won honor for
himself and his team, but he also won honor for his home
city. Often the city would build a special gate in his honor;
and when the hero came home, they would escort him
through it with great pomp and ceremony. Peter may have
had this thought in mind when he wrote, "For so an entrance shall be ministered unto you abundantly into the everlasting kingdom of our Lord and Savior Jesus Christ"
(2 Pet. 1:11). When the faithful Christian runner faces
death, he is not afraid; for death simply means an "abundant entrance" into God's presence, a glorious "Welcome
home!" in heaven.

"The thing that ultimately is going to test the value of
our professed Christian faith is the way in which we face
old age, is the way in which we face death," said Dr. D.
Martyn Lloyd-Jones. "When I come to be an old man, and
when I come to die, if I am truly Christian, death to me
will be but an entrance, an entrance into a glorious life"
(*Expository Sermons on 2 Peter*, pp. 49-50).

No matter how glorious may be the beginning of the
race, the important thing is how it ends. The late president
of Moody Bible Institute, Dr. William Culbertson, often
prayed, "Father, may we end well." The well-known British Bible teacher, Dr. F. B. Meyer, was greatly concerned
that his life "not end in a swamp." More than one person
in the Bible started gloriously but ended tragically: Lot,
Samson, Gideon, King Saul, King Uzziah, and Demas
come to mind. Of course, we want to end well and receive

the reward, not to boast, but to bring honor and glory to our Savior.

Finally, winning athletes *know how to practice teamwork*. Even a great Christian like Paul did not try to win the prize by himself. He had a number of associates in ministry who labored with him in the gospel. Barnabas and Mark accompanied him on his first missionary journey, and Silas and Timothy were his helpers on his second journey. Priscilla and Aquila helped him both in Corinth and in Ephesus, and Timothy and Titus were trusted allies who could be sent on special missions at a moment's notice. "Paul attracted friends around him as a magnet attracts iron filings," wrote Dr. F. F. Bruce. "There are about seventy people mentioned by name in the New Testament of whom we should never have heard were it not for their association with Paul" (*The Pauline Circle*, Eerdmans, 1985).

When Paul urged the believers in Philippi to "strive together for the faith of the gospel" (1:27), he was using a sports image. "Strive" comes from the Greek word *athleo*, which gives us the English word *athletic*. It means "to contend for a prize, to compete in the games." The prefix *sun-* means "together" and carries the idea of "teamwork." Paul pictured the local church as a team of athletes, striving together to reach their God-given goal.

The same word is translated "labored with" in Philippians 4:3. Euodia and Syntyche had been teammates with Paul when he started the church in Philippi. Now these two women were at odds with each other and creating problems for the rest of the team (4:2). Perhaps Paul had them in mind when he wrote, "Do nothing out of selfish ambition or vain conceit, but in humility consider others better than yourselves" (Phil. 2:3, NIV).

The successful team works together. There is no place for the "glory hound" who has to make all the points and get all the credit. What a rebuke this is to church members who split congregations or Sunday school classes because they cannot have their own way! In my own pastoral and itinerant ministry, I have met or heard about people who left the church because their names were accidentally left out of the bulletin or because they were not recognized from the platform. One man I know left a church because he was not elected to an office. The winning athlete thinks about the whole team and not just himself. He knows how to work together for the good of all his teammates.

The interesting thing about the "Christian team" is that we can all encourage one another, even after we have been called to glory. I am writing these words while seated in my library, surrounded by more than eight thousand books, many of them written by people who have been in heaven for many years. Yet these "teammates" are still encouraging me. They are like the believers listed in Hebrews 11, a "great cloud of witnesses" who are bearing witness to the church today that God does honor faith and enable us to win the race. The word *witnesses* in Hebrews 12:1 does not mean that they are watching from heaven. It means that they are bearing witness to us in the Old Testament that it is possible to "run the race with endurance" and win the prize.

But we cannot be good athletes merely by being spectators. If we are merely spectators, the only muscles we will develop are our eye muscles! (Well, maybe our vocal cords, too.) Somebody has defined a football game as an event in which thousands of people who need exercise pay for the privilege of cheering for twenty-two healthy men who need no exercise. Of course, it is much easier to be a spectator than a participant—except when the event is over and they give out the prizes.

Then we will wish we had gotten out of the stands and joined the team.

It isn't too late to start running.

CHAPTER 10

An Ambassador of the King

I n December 1814 William Carey's son Felix resigned from his missionary work to become ambassador in Calcutta for the king of Burma. While most parents would have been proud of this appointment, his father was deeply hurt and wrote home, "Felix is shriveled from a missionary into an ambassador." Events proved that this evaluation was correct, for seven months later, Felix was recalled in disgrace and had to flee into Assam for safety.

We as Christians are not required to make this choice because *every* believer is called by Christ to be both a missionary ("one who is sent") and an ambassador ("one who carries a message"). Jesus said, "As my Father hath sent me, even so send I you" (John 20:21). Paul wrote, "Now, then, we are ambassadors for Christ" (2 Cor. 5:20).

Some wit has defined an ambassador as a politician who did not get elected to office but was *given* an office on condition that he leave the country. In Bible times, the word *ambassador* had little to do with politics. Rather, it carried the meaning of "personal messenger," one sent on a special mission (2 Chron. 35:21; Isa. 18:1-2; Luke 14:32). The ambassador was under the authority of a ruler or a government official. He was sent to declare a message but not to negotiate the response.

In Paul's day Rome had two different kinds of provinces, each related to the Roman government in a different way. *Senatorial provinces* were made up of people who had submitted to Rome and were peacefully obeying the law. *Imperial provinces,* however, were still rebellious and would create problems for Rome if they could. Rome sent ambassadors to the imperial provinces but not to the senatorial provinces.

Christians are God's ambassadors to this world because the world is at war with God (Rom. 5:10; 8:5-8). Through the sacrifice of Jesus Christ on the cross, God has been reconciled to the world (2 Cor. 5:18-19); but the world will not repent and be reconciled to God. For this reason, God must deal with this rebellious world as Rome dealt with their imperial provinces. He must send his ambassadors with his message of peace. Indeed, even this is an act of grace; for God has every right to send his angelic armies and judge the world for its sin. Instead, he offers sinners the gift of peace and forgiveness.

What are the characteristics of an ambassador and how do they relate to us as God's ambassadors today?

To begin with, an ambassador must be *a citizen of the nation he or she represents.* While it is not unusual for an ambassador from one country to intervene and represent another country, especially when sensitive issues are involved (hostages, war, etc.), it is only the country's official ambassador who has the authority to act. He may consult with other leaders, and even ask for their assistance, but he alone can take the responsibility for whatever decisions are made.

All of God's ambassadors were once citizens of Satan's kingdom, living outside the kingdom of God. They could not leave Satan's realm in their own power, nor could they make themselves citizens of God's kingdom by their own efforts. Only Jesus Christ can set sinners free and give them new citizenship. "Who hath delivered us from the power [authority] of darkness, and hath translated us into the kingdom of his dear Son: in whom we have redemption through his blood, even the forgiveness of sins" (Col. 1:13-14).

The word translated *delivered* means "to rescue from danger" and is used in 2 Peter 2:7 to describe Lot's deliverance from Sodom. The word *translated* comes from a Greek word that means "to move defeated people from one land to another," such as the deportation of prisoners of war. When we trusted Jesus Christ, we were moved out of Satan's defeated kingdom and into the victorious kingdom of the Lord. It is a "deportation" that means glory and freedom, not shame and slavery. Because we are saved, we have been turned "from darkness to light, and from the power of Satan unto God" (Acts 26:18).

For God's ambassadors, their true citizenship ["conversation" in the King James Version] is in heaven (Phil. 3:20) and their names are written down in heaven (Luke 10:20; Phil. 4:3). This heavenly citizenship qualifies believers to represent the Father as ambassadors on earth.

Ambassadors *must be commissioned*. While sometimes private citizens may be influential in dealing with foreign powers, it is the official ambassador who has the authority to act. He is the one who has been commissioned by his government and whose credentials have been approved and accepted. "Free-lance ambassadors" usually produce good publicity but bad diplomacy.

Every Christian is an "ambassador for Christ" whether he knows it or not or even agrees with his calling. God has given to us "the ministry of reconciliation" and "the word of reconciliation" (2 Cor. 5:18-19), and we must, in Christ's stead, plead with a rebellious world to be reconciled to God. "As my Father hath sent me, so send I you" (John 20:21; and see John 17:18).

This means that our chief job in this world is to share the gospel and to seek to lead people to faith in Jesus Christ. We are God's ambassadors of peace. Contrary to what most people think, God has not declared war on this world. He has declared peace. Like the nation of Israel as they conquered the Promised Land, we declare God's peace to the enemy and give them the opportunity to surrender to the Lord (Deut. 20:10-12). We are commissioned by the King of Kings.

Third, an ambassador *represents his ruler and his people.* Not every believer is called to full-time Christian service, but every believer is called to full-time Christian living. No matter where we are, we represent Jesus Christ and his church; and people form their opinions of God and the gospel from what they see and hear in us. It is unfortunate that so many Christians act like tourists instead of like ambassadors and give the world a wrong image of the Christian faith.

On more than one occasion, my wife and I have been embarrassed by the behavior of some American tourists overseas. We watched one group almost desecrate Westminster Abbey by their loud conversation and laughter and their total disrespect for the monuments there. We met another discourteous group on a public bus, and we cringed and almost tried to hide our citizenship as they joked about the very nation that was showing hospitality to them. Between cheap TV shows and discourteous tourists, America manages to export the worst possible image.

The ambassador has no right to manufacture his message, for it is given to him by his ruler; and our message is the gospel of Jesus Christ (1 Cor. 15:1-8). To proclaim any other message is to invite the judgment of God (Gal. 1:1-9). "Be reconciled to God" is our constant plea as we come into contact with lost sinners.

The ambassador does not promote himself or allow his own personal interests to get in the way of his official work. "For we preach not ourselves, but Christ Jesus the Lord, and ourselves your servants for Jesus' sake" (2 Cor. 4:5). When the messenger becomes more important than the message, you have the beginnings of a cult; and that is always dangerous. We must bear in mind the words of Oswald Chambers: "The Holy Spirit will only witness to a testimony when Jesus Christ is exalted higher than the testimony."

We are *always* representing our King, and we must be certain that he is pleased with what we say and do. Being an ambassador is not a job that goes from eight to four each day. The ambassador is *always* the ambassador, and he or she must behave accordingly. David Hogg, David Livingstone's neighbor in Scotland, said to him, "Now, lad, make religion the everyday business of your life, not a thing of fits and starts." No wonder Livingstone was such a good ambassador.

The ambassador *has all of his or her needs provided.* This in itself bears witness to the glory and strength of the nation that commissioned the ambassador. If you have ever visited different embassies, then you know how easy it is to judge the nation by the things you see in the building.

"But my God shall supply all your need according to his riches in glory by Christ Jesus" (Phil. 4:19). He himself is our shield and our reward, our protection and provision (Gen. 15:1). As long as you and I are on the King's business, seeking to honor his name and do his will, he will see to it that we receive all that we need. There is no need for his ambassadors to worry, for all the resources of heaven and earth are at their disposal, and he himself is with them wherever they go (Matt. 28:18-20).

When the University of Glasgow honored David Livingstone with a Doctor of Laws degree, he told the assembly, " 'Lo, I am with you always, even unto the end of the world.' On those words I staked everything and they never failed. I was never left alone!"

An ambassador *keeps in touch with headquarters.* After all, he must know what his ruler is thinking and how his nation wants him to act concerning the important matters of state. This is especially true when enemies are at work and the country is in danger. Each nation has a "general policy" that expresses the official position on many matters. It also has a strategy for applying this policy in day-to-day decisions. All of this the ambassador must know.

God's "official statement" is found in the Bible. What he says there reveals his character, his purposes, and his methods of getting things done. As we read the Bible and meditate on it, we discover God's will and God's strategy for his people in this world. As we pray and wait before the Lord in worship, the Spirit uses the Word to guide us in our daily decisions. It is not necessary for us to "invent" anything. The strategy is given to us from heaven.

It is interesting to examine the "go" statements given by our Lord. We are to "go home" (Mark 5:19), go "into the streets and lanes of the city" (Luke 14:21), go "into the highways and hedges" (Luke 14:23), and go "into all the world" (Mark 16:15). Acts 1:8 outlines God's program: we start being ambassadors at home, and then we gradually reach out to a whole world. "The Spirit of Christ is the spirit of missions," said missionary Henry Martyn, "and the nearer we get to him, the more intensely missionary we must become."

The ambassador who does not keep in touch with head-quarters is in danger of jeopardizing his nation's foreign policy. No matter how popular or successful he may seem, his independent activities might even lead to war. He must not only work together with his leaders, but he must also work in harmony with other officials to make sure that he represents his nation well. This leads to another important characteristic of the ambassador.

The ambassador must *always be prepared to give account*. "For we must all appear before the judgment seat of Christ; that every one may receive the things done in his body, according to that he hath done, whether it be good or bad" (2 Cor. 5:10). It is not a question of the ambassador's citizenship but of his faithfulness, whether or not he or she faithfully obeyed orders and represented the nation well.

The judgment seat of Christ should not be confused with

the white throne judgment described in Revelation 20:11-
15, for that is a judgment of lost sinners. The judgment
seat of Christ is a judgment of the works (not sins) of God's
people, and its purpose is to determine the rewards that
will be given. While we do not serve God primarily to receive rewards, he graciously will give them to us if we
have been faithful in our service.

The word translated "appear" means "to be revealed." It
is translated "made manifest" in verse 11. What we really
are will be made known at the judgment seat of Christ
when the records are opened. It is interesting how often
the passing of time changes the historian's evaluation of
world figures. Why? Because more facts are discovered en-
abling the historian to have a better perspective of his subject. "Therefore, judge nothing before the time, until the
Lord come, who both will bring to light the hidden things
of darkness, and will make manifest the counsels of the
hearts: and then shall every man have praise of God"
(1 Cor. 4:5). A wise warning to heed!

Each believer's works will be judged by the Lord, and
those that were faithfully done for his glory will be rewarded. Just as human leaders bestow medals and tro-
phies for meritorious service, so our Father will recognize
his faithful ambassadors. These rewards are identified in
Scripture as "crowns" (1 Cor. 9:25; 2 Tim. 4:8; James 1:12;
1 Pet. 5:4; Rev. 2:10 and 3:11). However, God's ambassadors will not claim their crowns for themselves. Rather,
they will give them in worship and adoration to their King
of Kings (Rev. 4:10).

The fact that we shall one day stand before Christ's
judgment seat ought to encourage us to be faithful. It
should also encourage us to avoid passing judgment on
others (Rom. 14:10-23). Only God can see the human
heart, and only God can pass righteous judgment. The
ministry that we may think is deeply spiritual may in reality be very carnal, and a ministry that we think is unimportant may be one of the most important in God's kingdom.

It is dangerous to pass judgment "before the time."

What is the reward that we really want? "Wherefore, we labour, that, whether present [with the Lord] or absent, we may be accepted of him" (2 Cor. 5:9). The word translated "accepted" means "well pleasing." Believers are already "accepted in the beloved" (Eph. 1:6), and that takes care of their salvation. But we want to live and serve in such a way that we are well pleasing to him. We all want to hear him say, "Well done, thou good and faithful servant" (Matt. 25:21). Knowing that we have brought joy to the Father's heart is reward enough.

Ambassadors are expected to *obey the laws of the land and the orders given to them.* If an ambassador flouts the law and refuses to obey, his commission is taken from him and he is removed from his high office. He does not cease to be a citizen of his nation, but he does cease to enjoy the privileges and powers of the office. When a Christian disobeys God, he or she does not cease to belong to God's family and God's kingdom. But that Christian does forfeit the joys and privileges of the Christian ambassador.

Jonah is a classic example of a disobedient ambassador. God called Jonah to go to the Gentile city of Nineveh and warn them that judgment was coming. Being a prejudiced man, Jonah had no desire to see the hated Gentile Ninevites spared; so he went in the opposite direction and refused to obey God's call.

How did God deal with Jonah? He disciplined him until he finally yielded to the Lord and obeyed his will, at least outwardly. Jonah did not cease to be God's child when he was in rebellion, but he did cease to enjoy God's blessing. He did not forfeit his citizenship, but he did forfeit his joy, his peace, and his effectiveness as a witness.

As God's ambassadors, we are not responsible for the way people respond to the message. Our task is to obey God's will and faithfully deliver his Word. His task is to use that Word to accomplish his divine purposes (Isa. 55:8-11). Wherever the Apostle Paul ministered, some people believed, others delayed, and some openly opposed the message. He was a faithful ambassador who left the results with the Lord.

Ambassadors are usually *called home before war is declared.* The Lord Jesus Christ has promised to return to take his people home to heaven (John 14:1-6; 1 Thess. 4:13-18). While good and godly students of the Bible may not agree on the details of prophecy, they do agree that Jesus is coming again and that his coming will be sudden. After his people have been taken to glory, God will send judgment on the earth (see 1 Thess. 5:1-11).

While I do not make it a test of fellowship or spirituality, I believe that the church will be caught up *before* God pours his wrath upon the world. We have put our faith in "Jesus, who delivered us from the wrath to come" (1 Thess. 1:10). "For God hath not appointed us to wrath but to obtain salvation by our Lord Jesus Christ" (1 Thess. 5:9).

As long as God's ambassadors are in this world, God is calling sinners to repent and believe the gospel. We are "declaring peace" and asking sinners to be reconciled to God. But there will come a day when God will call his ambassadors home, and then he will declare war. This does not mean that people cannot be saved during that time of terrible tribulation, but they will have to pay a great price for their testimony (Rev. 7:9-17).

The world persecutes God's ambassadors. It does not realize that the very presence of God's people in this world is their opportunity for salvation and hope. After the ambassadors are called out of this world, the wrath of God will fall; and this will mean death and eternal judgment for many people.

If you have never trusted Jesus Christ as your Savior, "behold, now is the accepted time; behold, now is the day of salvation" (2 Cor. 6:2). Trust him today! You cannot be sure of tomorrow.

If you are one of his children, then you are also an ambassador for Jesus Christ. Be a faithful ambassador! Share his message with the lost world while there is still opportunity. Help others carry the message where you cannot go.

"How long have you had the Glad Tidings in England?" a Chinese Christian asked Hudson Taylor.

Somewhat embarrassed, Taylor told him that England had known the gospel for several hundred years.

"What!" exclaimed the man. "Several hundreds of years! Is it possible that you have known about Jesus so long and only now have come to tell us? My father sought the truth for more than twenty years and died without finding it. Oh, why did you not come sooner?"

How would you answer that question?

CHAPTER 11

Seeds and Loaves of Bread

When we study Bible types and symbols, we must take care not to make one symbol always mean the same thing. Our present study is a case in point. In our Lord's "Parable of the Tares," the seed represents God's people and the field represents the world. In the "Parable of the Sower," the seed represents the Word of God and the soil pictures different kinds of human hearts. We must not get the two confused.

1. God's People Are Seeds

Why would the Lord Jesus compare the children of God to seeds? For one thing, *seeds contain life*. We can manufacture golf balls or even diamonds, but we cannot manufacture seeds. They are the product of life.

Christians possess eternal life, the very life of God. "He who believes in the Son has everlasting life; and he who does not believe the Son shall not see life, but the wrath of God abides on him" (John 3:36, NKJV). This life is a gift, and the gift is received by faith in the Savior, the Son of God (John 17:2-3).

One of the main lessons of this parable is that *Satan*

tries to imitate this life. Wherever in this world God plants true believers, Satan comes and plants the counterfeit. Satan is not an originator; he is an imitator (see 2 Cor. 11:13-16, 26). Jesus warned us that on the day of judgment many people will be surprised to discover that they were never truly saved (Matt. 7:21-23).

Christians are like seeds in that *they are small but powerful*. A seed is a relatively small and weak thing. But when we plant it, power is released and the roots go downward while the shoots move upward. A growing tree can send its roots into the foundation of a house and crack the foundation. Growing plants have been known to overcome great obstacles as they reach toward the sun.

Perhaps we are the only Christian in our family or in our office, and we may feel quite inadequate. We need to remember that we share the very power of God, and that his power working through us can accomplish great things (Eph. 1:17-23; 3:20-21). The saints have always been a minority; but if we plant enough seeds, we will get a harvest.

Seeds produce fruit, and fruit has in it the seeds for more fruit (John 15:1-8). God expects us to "reproduce ourselves" as we minister in this world. God is looking for the fruit of the Spirit (Gal. 5:22-23) as we grow in Christian character. He yearns for us to win others to the Savior (Rom. 1:13) and to be "fruitful in every good work" (Col. 1:10). God is looking for a harvest from each life.

This leads to an important truth: *seeds must be planted before there can be a harvest*. Jesus said, "Most assuredly I say to you, unless a grain of wheat falls into the ground and dies, it remains alone; but if it dies, it produces much grain" (John 12:24, NKJV). This is another way of saying, "If any one desires to come after Me, let him deny himself, and take up his cross, and follow Me. For whoever desires to save his life will lose it, and whoever loses his life for My sake will find it" (Matt. 16:24-25, NKJV).

It is a relatively easy matter to deny *things*, but it is

painful to deny *self*. In fact, many of us deny things as a substitute for the real sacrifice God wants, denying ourselves (Rom. 12:1-2). Our Lord compared himself to a seed, and his sacrifice on the cross to the planting of that seed into the ground. He had to die before he could be fruitful in resurrection "newness of life" (Rom. 6:4). If a seed could speak, it would no doubt protest against the darkness and death of its earthly "grave," but how else could it produce a harvest?

A believer visiting a mission field said to one of the dedicated workers, "My, you certainly are buried out here!" The missionary quietly replied, "We were not buried—we were planted! We buried ourselves long before we ever arrived on this field."

Seeds reveal the wisdom of God and the variety of God's people. There are many varieties of seeds, yet all of them have a place in God's great world. Some seeds are tiny, while others are large. It takes 35 million seeds of the *Epiphytic* orchid to make one ounce! Some seeds are very light and fragile, while others are protected by a strong husk. There are seeds that have sails and blow in the wind, and there are seeds that have burrs and stick to our clothes. In his wisdom, God designed each seed perfectly so it would do the job he gave it to do.

We have a tendency in our churches to want to "manufacture" carbon-copy, cookie-cutter Christians. But God delights in variety! It would be wrong to compare the sunflower seed, rich in oil, with the tiny orchid seed that is barely visible. And we would be questioning the wisdom of God. Yes, all believers should become more like Jesus Christ. But when we do that, it brings out our own individuality that much more. Peter did not become like John; he retained his own distinctive personality and was used by the Lord in his own special ministry. God knows just where to plant his seeds so that they will do the most good.

It's rather obvious, but *seeds must be scattered*. Jesus

Christ is the Lord of the harvest, and he scatters his seeds according to his perfect plan. Sometimes he uses persecution to scatter believers and get the gospel into new places. When Saul of Tarsus was opposing the church, he thought he was *destroying* God's witness, when actually he was *extending* it! "At that time [when Stephen was martyred] a great persecution arose against the church which was at Jerusalem; and they were all scattered" (Acts 8:1). "Therefore those who were scattered went everywhere preaching the word" (Acts 8:4).

The Greek word translated *scattered* means "to sow seed." The difficult winds of persecution only spread the message abroad and allowed it to take root in other fields. In fact, some of the "Christian seeds" went to Antioch and started a new church (Acts 11:19ff.); and it was that church that later commissioned Paul to take the message to the Gentiles (Acts 13:1ff.)! How wonderful are the ways of God!

2. The Church Is a Loaf of Bread
"Do you not know that a little leaven leavens the whole lump?" (1 Cor. 5:6, NKJV). "For we, being many, are one bread" (1 Cor. 10:17, NKJV).

While each individual seed must be planted, the seeds must also be united as "one loaf," the church. Paul compared the church at Corinth to a loaf of bread, and for several reasons.

To begin with, *bread is made from grain.* As we have just seen, believers are seeds. But in order to produce a loaf of bread, we must grind the grain and make flour, mix the dough, and bake the loaf in the oven. Christians should be the kind of people who know what it is to be "ground" by God and put through the furnace of affliction. The loaf of bread illustrates the fact that believers must let God break them and unite them.

Paul saw the loaf as a symbol of unity. "For we, being

many, are one bread and one body" (1 Cor. 10:17). A jar full of individual seeds is not a picture of unity. When that grain is crushed and baked into a loaf, then we have a true picture of unity. Too many churches are nothing but jars of grain. God wants to crush that grain and put the dough into the furnace so he can make a loaf that is united to his glory.

The purpose of bread, of course, is *to feed others*. The bread does not eat itself! The church is in the world to feed hungry sinners and share with them the eternal life that only Jesus Christ can give. We are something like the bread that Jesus gave to his disciples to share with the five thousand and the four thousand. We must be broken and handed out, or we do no good. "For whoever desires to save his life will lose it" (Matt. 16:25).

One of the most important lessons we learn from the loaf is that *the dough must be pure*. In 1 Corinthians 5, Paul used an illustration that was familiar to every Jew and to many Gentiles, the purging of the leaven at Passover (see Exod. 12:15-20). The Jews were not permitted to have yeast (leaven) in their bread at Passover, nor was there to be any leaven anywhere in their dwellings. Leaven was a symbol of evil. It is small, but it spreads rapidly; it permeates the dough; and it puffs up (1 Cor. 4:6, 18-19; 5:2).

In the context of 1 Corinthians 5, the "leaven" was a member of the church who was living in sin, and everybody knew about it. Because the man would not repent and forsake his shameful sin, Paul told them to discipline the rebel and put him out of the assembly. Just as yeast spreads and affects the whole lump, so one disobedient believer can poison a whole church.

Church discipline is not a popular activity. Most church leaders shun it. But just as loving discipline is good for our children, so it is good for God's people. Paul told them to discipline the man *for his own sake* (vv. 1-5), so that he might repent and not have to feel the disciplining rod of God. But Paul also said that the church should discipline

him *for the church's sake* (vv. 6-8), so that the evil influence of the man might not infect others. In verses 9-13,
Paul pointed out that church discipline was also *for the
world's sake.* How can a polluted church bear witness to a
lost world? If the people in the church are no different
from the people in the world, then the world will never
pay attention to the church's message.

Leaven is not only a picture of "malice and wickedness"
(1 Cor. 5:8), it is also a picture of hypocrisy. "Beware of the
leaven of the Pharisees, which is hypocrisy" (Luke 12:1).
The word *hupokrites* means "an actor, a pretender." In
Greek drama, the actors wore masks instead of makeup to
depict the various persons in the story. When a believer de-
liberately starts to pretend, then he is practicing the sin of
hypocrisy; and he is starting to "leaven" the fellowship.

Jesus also used leaven to illustrate *false doctrine.* "Take
heed and beware of the leaven of the Pharisees and the
Sadducees. . . . Then they understood that he did not tell
them to beware of the leaven of bread, but of the doctrine
of the Pharisees and Sadducees" (Matt. 16:6, 12; see also
Gal. 5:7-9).

The false doctrine of the Pharisees was *legalism*, thinking that by keeping certain standards and obeying certain
rules, they were automatically right with God (Luke 18:9-
14; see also Matt. 23). The Sadducees did not believe in
angels, spirits, or the resurrection (Acts 23:6-8). They were
the antisupernaturalists of their day and rejected all of the
Old Testament Scriptures except the five books of Moses.

It does not take long for false doctrine to quietly spread
like leaven in a local church fellowship. In fact, lies seem
to increase faster than truth. We can visit churches and
schools that were once true to the faith, but today they
deny, and even laugh at, that "apostolic faith" that they
once affirmed.

I once visited a famous church in London, pastored at
one time by a courageous evangelical preacher. "If the gospel ceases to be preached from this pulpit," he once shout-

ed, "I hope somebody will write 'Ichabod' above the door!" (*Ichabod* is Hebrew for "the glory has departed." See 1 Sam. 4:21.) The very next pastor the church installed preached what he called "the new theology," an attractive form of liberalism. The leaven began to grow; and, one day, somebody *did* write "Ichabod" over the door of the church.

There is also the leaven of *worldliness and compromise.* Jesus called this "the leaven of Herod" (Mark 8:15; see also Mark 6:17-29). Herod Antipas was a godless man who wanted to be known as a faithful Jew. Yet he killed John the Baptist, the greatest of the prophets. He sought to please people and maintain his popularity, and all the time his character was eroding. When God's people compromise with evil and seek to cater to the world, they are introducing leaven into the loaf (see 2 Cor. 6:14–7:1).

If the church is to be the kind of bread that can indeed feed a starving world, it must maintain its purity of doctrine and purity of practice. We must take to heart passages like 1 Timothy 4 and 2 Timothy 3, as well as Paul's warning to the leaders of the Ephesian church (Acts 20:28-35). The famous British preacher Dr. G. Campbell Morgan used to say that the church did the most for the world when the church was the most unlike the world.

3. Personal Inventory

The image we have just studied presents the believer as an individual and also as a part of the church, the seed and the loaf. It is important that we apply these truths personally so that we might help make the church all that God wants it to be. Here are some "inventory questions" we might ask ourselves regularly.

1. Do I truly have God's life within me? Am I a "living seed"?
2. Do I realize the great power and potential that is within me because of the grace of God?

3. Am I planted where he wants me? Am I seeking to bear fruit right where I am, or am I complaining and seeking a "better" place?
4. Am I willing to die to self so that the fruit might come?
5. Am I a living part of the local church fellowship? Is our church truly a united "loaf," and not just a collection of seeds?
6. Do I strive to keep the leaven out of my life?
7. Am I willing to risk popularity in order to keep the leaven out of our fellowship?
8. Am I under the authority of my church and will I support biblical church discipline?
9. Is our church feeding others or just existing for itself?

CHAPTER 12

The New Creation

"The new age is coming!"
"The new world is just around the corner!"
"Are you ready for the new society?"

Slogans like these have been bombarding us in recent years, with books, seminars, and rallies promoting them. People who believe this "new age" message are spending a lot of money to get ready. If only the world would realize that the "new age" has been here for nearly two thousand years, and that it is just as exciting today as it was when it first broke into history!

God's "new age" burst on the scene when Jesus Christ came into the world and completed the work of redemption. He died for the sins of the world, he arose from the dead, and he returned to heaven and sent the Holy Spirit to his people. All who trust Jesus Christ are "in him" and are a part of God's "new age." Paul wrote: "Therefore, if anyone is in Christ, he is a new creation; old things have passed away; behold, all things have become new" (2 Cor. 5:17, NKJV).

Not "all things *ought to be* new," but "all things have become new." The "new creation" is not a dream for tomorrow; it is a dynamic reality for today. If you are a Christian, then you are not only in God's "new creation," but *you yourself are a "new creation!"* In order to grasp this truth and be able to put it to work in your life, you must understand God's three creations.

1. The Old Creation—Illustration (Gen. 1)

Paul used the word *creation* because he wanted us to see the parallel between salvation and the creative work of God as recorded in Genesis 1. After all, Christians are "his workmanship, created in Christ Jesus" (Eph. 2:10). Notice the comparisons that help us better understand what it means to be God's "new creation."

Creation begins with God. "In the beginning God created the heavens and the earth" (Gen. 1:1). Salvation begins with God, and he had it planned long before he made the universe (Eph. 1:4; Rev.13:8). The prophet Jonah said it perfectly: "Salvation is of the Lord!" (2:9). When we ponder the truth that God thought of us eternities before we were born, it makes us appreciate the marvel of his grace. Of course, whatever God begins, he finishes (Phil. 1:6); so the "new creation" is going to succeed. God planned salvation, God provided it and paid for it, and God will perform all that is needed to fulfill his wonderful plan.

Creation involves the Holy Spirit. "And the Spirit of God was hovering over the face of the waters" (Gen. 1:2, NKJV). Apart from the ministry of the Holy Spirit, no sinner could ever be saved. It is the Spirit who convicts us of sin (John 16:7-11) and reveals the Savior to us. We are born again through the power of God's Spirit (John 3:1-8), and that same Spirit witnesses to us and assures us that we are the children of God (Rom. 8:9, 14-17).

Notice the condition of things when the Spirit went to work: darkness, emptiness, and formlessness (Gen. 1:2). What a picture of the lost sinner! In the six days of creation, the Lord *formed* and then *filled*. The sequence was like this:

The Spirit formed	*The Spirit filled*
Day 1: light	Day 4: lights (sun, moon)
Day 2: firmament, water	Day 5: birds and fish
Day 3: land, plants	Day 6: man and animals

When we are a part of God's "new creation," the Spirit is at work in our lives, to form us and to fill us. Most of us enjoy the filling, but we don't like the forming! However, both are necessary if we are to become all that he wants us to become.

Creation involves God's Word. Nine times in the creation story we find the phrase "God said." God accomplishes his will through his Word. "By the word of the Lord were the heavens made. . . . For he spake, and it was done; he commanded, and it stood fast" (Ps. 33:6, 9). The Spirit of God uses the Word of God to convict sinners (Acts 2:37), to impart faith (Rom. 10:17), and to give life (John 5:24) to those who trust the Savior. He also uses the Word to transform the lives of the God's people and conform them to Christ (Eph. 5:26-27).

Creation involves light. "Let there be light!" (Gen. 1:3) was what got creation moving, and Paul saw in that a picture of our salvation. "For it is the God who commanded light to shine out of darkness who has shone in our hearts to give the light of the knowledge of the glory of God in the face of Jesus Christ" (2 Cor. 4:6, NKJV). If the light of life has not entered our hearts, then we are still in the darkness of sin and not a part of the "new creation" (John 1:6-13).

Creation requires a leader. God gave Adam and Eve dominion over creation (Gen. 1:26-28) and Adam headship over the human race. The old creation was headed up by the "first Adam," made from the earth; and the "new creation" is headed up by Jesus Christ, "the last Adam," who came from heaven (1 Cor. 15:45-49). Because God tested and judged the whole human race in Adam, he could then make salvation available to the whole human race through the Last Adam, Christ (Rom. 5:12-21).

The first Adam was tested in a perfect garden (except for the presence of Satan), and he failed. The Last Adam was tested in a wilderness, and he was victorious (Matt.

4:1-11). The first Adam was a thief who was cast out of Paradise. The Last Adam said to a thief, "Assuredly, I say to you, today you will be with Me in Paradise" (Luke 23:43, NKJV). When you trusted Jesus Christ to save you, you were born again and came under the headship of the Last Adam; and that makes you a "new creation." Unsaved people are "in Adam." Saved people are "in Christ."

Creation was all of grace. Before God made the first man and woman, he prepared for them everything that they would need. What grace! But the same thing is true in the "new creation." When we were born into God's family, we were born "complete in him [Jesus Christ]" (Col. 2:10). We were saved by grace (Eph. 2:8-9), and we must live by grace (1 Cor. 15:10), drawing upon the riches of his grace (Eph. 2:7; Phil. 4:19). When we are "in Christ," we have all that he is and all that he has available to us by faith.

Creation glorifies God. "The heavens declare the glory of God" (Ps. 19:1). Sin has certainly taken its toll on God's creation, but we can still see and admire his wisdom and power. The purpose of the "new creation" is that God be glorified throughout all eternity. What God has done for us in Jesus Christ is "to the praise of the glory of his grace" (Eph. 1:6, 12, 14). Our task as people living in the "new creation" is to see to it that everything we do brings glory to God (1 Cor. 6:19-20; Matt. 5:16).

God's "old creation" is a marvelous illustration of his "new creation." We should remember that the next time we watch a beautiful sunset or get caught in a sudden storm. God speaks to us not only through the written Word but also through the great book of nature, his "old creation."

2. God's New Creation—Application (2 Cor. 5)

When Paul wrote 2 Corinthians 5:17, he not only made a comparison but he also drew a conclusion. Notice that the verse begins with "therefore." A careful reading of the entire chapter reveals what Paul was getting across. If we are a part of the "new creation," then everything about us is new. We may not see it or understand it, and we may not always live like it; but everything is new just the same.

We find Paul emphasizing the same truth several times (Eph. 4:17ff.; Col. 3:1ff.). In these passages he wrote about the "old man" and the "new man," but the message was the same. He did not tell us to change our way of living so that God may accept us into his "new creation." He told us that God has already made us "new creations" in Christ, and this changes our way of living. The old man is buried with Christ. We have been raised from the dead and the graveclothes are left behind. "Behold, all things have become new!"

People who are in God's "new creation" look at life in a different way from those who still belong to the "old creation." This is the main message of 2 Corinthians 5.

To begin with, we look at *suffering and death* from God's point of view (5:1-8). We know that life is temporary (he compares the human body to a tent), and that the longer we live, the closer we get to death. But we are not afraid of death because death is our doorway into the presence of the Lord. This does not mean that Christians *court* death, but that they do not fear it.

We also have a different attitude toward *life and service* (5:9-11), for our motive for living and serving is to please God. We know that one day our works will be judged at the judgment seat of Christ, and this will determine our rewards (1 Cor. 3:5-17; Rom. 14:10-13). We see life as a stewardship of gifts, abilities, and opportunities; and we want to be faithful stewards (1 Cor. 4:2).

Because we are in the "new creation," we see *ourselves* in a new way (5:12-15). If people think we are "crazy," it doesn't upset us because our chief concern is to please God. (Note Acts 26:24; Mark 3:20-21; John 10:20.) When we belong to the "new creation," we soon discover that the "old creation" crowd does not understand us. We realize that Christ died for us *so that we may live for him*. People in the "old creation" live for themselves; people in the "new creation" live for Christ and for others.

We not only see ourselves in a new way, but we also see *Christ* in a new way (5:16). To know Christ "after the flesh" means to know him only as a human being in history, but not to know him as Savior and Lord. No doubt Paul knew many facts about Jesus Christ before he met the Savior personally, but what a difference it made when Paul said, "Lord, what do you want me to do?" (Acts 9:6, NKJV).

But this also means seeing *other people* in a new way (5:18-21). Those who belong to God's "new creation" evaluate people on the basis of a whole new standard, a *spiritual* standard. The fundamental matter is no longer "Jew or Gentile?" or "rich or poor?" but "saved or lost?" The Christian sees a world of lost sinners who need to be reconciled to God. If we are "new creation" people, then the way we read the newspaper or watch the news, and the way we do our job each day, is governed by "the ministry of reconciliation." Our great task in life is to bring sinners back to God. "We are ambassadors for Christ."

When a "new creation" person drops into some situation in the "old creation," there will often be conflict, because darkness hates light and selfishness despises love. Whether it is Joseph in Egypt, Moses in Pharaoh's court, Daniel in a pagan palace, Paul and Silas in a Roman prison, or Jesus Christ in the Jewish temple, something has to change. Why? Because "new creation" people are *transformers* and not *conformers* (Rom. 12:1-2). The power of God is at work in and through their lives, and their lives make a difference in the situation.

Of course, there is always the danger that the "old creation" will win the victory because the "new creation" fails to draw upon the divine resources available from the glorified Christ. When that happens, the *transformer* becomes "conformed to this world" (Rom. 12:2) and starts to live like the people in the "old creation." Compromise leads to conformity and conformity leads to defeat. It is when the believer is separated from sin (2 Cor. 6:14–7:1) that he or she exerts the greatest influence for God.

3. God's Future Creation—Anticipation

Where will it all end? With a glorious new heaven and earth that will be the perfect eternal home for God's "new creation" people. We find this future creation described in Revelation 21–22. In fact, we find in the Book of Revelation the victorious completion of all that God started in the Book of Genesis.

Genesis	Revelation
Heavens and earth, 1:1	New heavens and earth, 21:1
The sun created, 1:16	The sun not needed, 21:23
The night designated, 1:5	No night there, 22:5
Rivers on earth, 2:10-14	A river in heaven, 22:1-2
No access to tree of life, 3:24	Access to tree of life, 22:14
A curse, 3:14-17	No more curse, 22:3
Death, 3:19	No more death, 21:4
Sorrow, 3:17	No more sorrow, 21:4
Marriage of Adam, 2:8-23	Marriage of the Lamb, 19:1-8
The serpent deceives, 3:1ff.	The serpent judged, 20:10

There are more contrasts that might be made, but these will give you an idea of what is in store for God's "new creation."

Because of Adam's fall, the "old creation" is now in bondage and travail and is a "groaning" creation. But when the Savior returns in power, he will deliver his creation and make it a glorious creation (Rom. 8:18-25). Believers, too, will be delivered and will experience the redemption of the body (Rom. 8:23). God will give his people new bodies perfectly suited to the new environment of glory. What a day that will be! Best of all, we will be like the Lord Jesus Christ (1 John 3:1-2) and serve him forever.

Generally speaking, God today is not working on the

"redemption" of the old creation. To be sure, he can and does heal our bodies when it is his will. But the final redemption of the body awaits the return of the Savior. God can work through his people to make this world a safer and better place in which to live, but the new heaven and new earth can come only from the hand of God. We are not going to "bring in the kingdom" because the King will bring it in when he returns (Rev. 11:15-18).

Then what is God doing today? He is using the people of his "new creation" to touch the lives of people in the "old creation" and to urge them to "be reconciled to God" (2 Cor. 5:20). He is transforming his "new creation" people to make them more and more like his Son, and, in so doing, is bringing about moral and spiritual changes in this world. The light is dispelling darkness and the salt is retarding decay (Matt. 5:13-16).

Yes, the "new age" is here! God's people are already "living in kingdom come," as Vance Havner used to say. We are living in the future tense because we have forgotten "those things which are behind" and are "reaching forward to those things which are ahead" (Phil. 3:13, NKJV). God has already glorified us (Rom. 8:30; John 17:22); we are just waiting for that glory to be revealed at the coming of our Lord Jesus Christ (Rom. 8:17-19).

God's people are "the community of the new creation."

What a privilege!

What a responsibility!

What a future!